W9-BYX-364

Historical American Biographies

CARRY A. NATION

Saloon Smasher and Prohibitionist

Bonnie Carman Harvey

Enslow Publishers, Inc.

40 Industrial Road	PO Box 38
Box 398	Aldershot
Berkeley Heights, NJ 07922	Hants GU12 6BP
USA	UK

http://www.enslow.com

Library of Congress Cataloging-in-Publication Data

Harvey, Bonnie Carman
    Carry A. Nation : Saloon Smasher and Prohibitionist / Bonnie Carman
    Harvey.
        p. cm. — (Historical American biographies)
    Includes bibliographical references and index.
    Summary: Examines the life of Carry Nation, whose destruction of
saloons and other businesses that sold liquor in the late nineteenth and
early twentieth century won her both praise and criticism from fellow
prohibitionists and temperance workers.
    ISBN 0-7660-1907-1
    1. Nation, Carry Amelia, 1846-1911—Juvenile literature.
    2. Prohibitionists—United States—Biography—Juvenile literature.
    [1. Nation, Carry Amelia, 1846-1911. 2. Reformers. 3. Prohibition.
    4. Women—Biography. 5. Woman's Christian Temperance Union.]
    I. Title. II. Series.
    HV5232.N3 H37   2002
    363.4'1'092—dc21

                                        2001007431

Printed in the United States of America

10 9 8 7 6 5 4 3 2

To Our Readers: We have done our best to make sure all Internet Addresses in
this book were active and appropriate when we went to press. However, the
author and the publisher have no control over and assume no liability for the
material available on those Internet sites or on other Web sites they may link to.
Any comments or suggestions can be sent by e-mail to comments@enslow.com or
to the address on the back cover.

Illustration Credits: Enslow Publishers, Inc., p. 51; Kansas State
Historical Society, pp. 4, 7, 26, 40, 57, 63, 67, 76, 77, 80, 92, 98, 101,
102, 103, 108, 112.

Cover Illustration: Kansas State Historical Society, (Nation portrait and
background).

CONTENTS

Carry A. Nation

1

SALOON SMASHING

In June 1900, the customers in Jasper Dobson's speakeasy (or saloon) in Kiowa, Kansas, were stunned to see a sober-faced, middle-aged woman come through the front doors. Her dark clothing appeared appropriate only for Sunday-morning church. Soon, the 175-pound woman, Carry Nation, swung into action, hurling bricks and rocks in every direction and smashing the saloon's bottles, glassware, and furnishings.

Dobson tried to stop her, but Nation said,

> I told you last spring to close this place, Mr. Dobson, and you did not do it. Now I have come here with another remonstrance (earnest presentation of reasons for opposition). Get out of the way. I do not

want to strike you, but I am going to break this place up.[1]

While Nation sang verses from several hymns, she proceeded to wreck bar fixtures, glass, and everything else in sight. In the meantime, Dobson escaped to a corner and kept quiet to try to prevent the angry woman from turning on him. As she finally finished her tirade, she turned to him with a nod and swept out the door singing one of her favorite battle songs: "Who hath sorrow? Who hath woe? They who dare not answer no. They whose feet to sin incline, While they tarry [[linger in expectation)]] at the wine."[2]

Walking vigorously down the street, Nation swung into another saloon, known as Lewis's. She then proceeded to wreck it before the eyes of the astonished bartender and owner. The fearful customers fled through the back door, and Nation called to the young bartender: "Young man, come from behind that bar! Your mother did not raise you for such a place!"[3] Nation threw a brick at the mirror behind the bar, and the man quickly decided to obey her command. He, too, ran for the back door.

When Nation emerged a short time later, a crowd had gathered in the street.

She spoke to the crowd, telling them that she had destroyed three of their saloons. She said, "If I have broken a statute of Kansas, put me in jail. If I am

Mirrors were just one of Carry Nation's many targets for smashing. It was her way of sending a message to Kansas saloon owners to stop illegally selling liquor.

not a law-breaker, your Mayor and Councilmen are."[4] A number of city officials were in the crowd, and one of them asked her whether she thought they could take care of their own business. She said they could, but they would not because the officials looked the other way rather than close down the saloons. Nation then climbed into her buggy, yanked on the reins of her horse, Prince, and went home.

Earlier, in the summer of 1894, Nation set out to do battle against the saloons and other places that sold alcohol. Her target was Medicine Lodge, Kansas. As she marched down the street in the Kansas town, her face showed determination. A Baptist minister's wife, Kate Cain, accompanied Nation in her march toward Medicine Lodge's biggest saloon, or "joint," owned by Mart Strong.

In the mid-1890s, Nation and Cain had formed a local chapter of the Women's Christian Temperance Union (WCTU) in Medicine Lodge. Nation was chosen to be the jail evangelist. As jail evangelist, Nation soon discovered that many of the prisoners were in jail because of alcohol-related offenses.

Although states like Massachusetts (1838) and New York (1845) had passed laws enabling local governments to prohibit alcohol, the laws were not always effective. The state of Maine became the first state to approve a statewide prohibition law in 1851.[5]

Kansas, too, had been a legally "dry" state since 1880. Nevertheless, many places continued to serve alcohol in secret. These places that served illegal alcohol were called "joints." Nation believed it was now time to take strong action against the sale of alcoholic beverages.

A Prohibition party was founded in 1869 in the United States. Twenty years later, in the 1892 presidential election, the party's candidate, General John Bidwell, received 271,000 votes (out of 12 million cast), the party's best showing until that time.

Nation's decision to take matters into her own hands concerning the sale of alcohol resulted from her marriage in her early twenties to an alcoholic. She had always been against alcohol, but she became much more active in crusading against it in 1890. That year, the U.S. Supreme Court passed a law favoring the importation and sale of alcohol in original packages from state to state. This decision meant that the transactions were subject only to interstate commerce laws. When Nation learned of the Court's decision, she was outraged because it considerably weakened the prohibition laws of Kansas.

Now, in 1894, all the thoughts about alcohol's terrible effects on the family raced through Nation's mind as she headed toward Strong's Medicine Lodge saloon. Once in front of the joint, Nation spoke to the crowd gathered around her: "Men and women of Medicine Lodge, this is a joint! Let us pray!"[6]

Then Nation pushed her way through the swinging doors into Strong's saloon. Mart Strong was waiting for her and grabbed hold of her in the front room. He turned her around and shoved her back out the front door, saying, "Get out of here, you crazy woman!"[7] After a few minutes, Nation tried to go back in, but Strong gave her a hard shove, and she fell down. Strong closed and locked his saloon doors. Nation, and the two hundred or so women who had gathered around her, moved to the Medicine Lodge mayor's home, demanding that Strong's joint be closed for good. The next morning Nation learned that Strong had left town. He would not return.

Six more joints remained open in Medicine Lodge. Nation and the women marched to Harry Durst's joint next. Just outside, the women began praying in loud voices. The customers inside, hearing the women, scattered in all directions because they knew Nation was near. Durst was left alone to face Nation. When he stepped outside, she caught hold of him, screaming that he was going to hell. Before long, he fled both Medicine Lodge and Kansas.

In 1900, Nation turned her attention to Hank O'Bryan's place. To Nation's delight, a short time after she marched on O'Bryan's saloon, he closed its doors. Three weeks later, she learned that city officials had closed three more joints.

Despite her many victories in closing saloons, Nation paid a price. Her home was vandalized. Her windows were broken. She received threats that her home would be set on fire. Someone cut her horse's harness causing the wreck of the buggy she was riding in. Although Nation experienced these setbacks, she also began to have favor with city officials. In 1895, the Barber County WCTU elected her as its president. Finally she had won recognition from the organization.

Following Nation's attacks on saloons in various Kansas towns, the Wichita and Topeka papers carried brief reports about her raids. Many women from all over Kansas wrote her and praised her for

The Women's Christian Temperance Union
The Women's Christian Temperance Union (WCTU) was founded when seventeen state delegates from the Woman's Crusade met in Cleveland and pledged their allegiance to a new organization on November 7, 1874. They formed temperance (antialcohol) leagues and committed themselves to the cause of closing saloons across the country. The group nominated and elected Annie Wittenmyer, a celebrated Civil War nurse, as its first president. Five years later, the group elected Frances Willard as its president. She retained the position until her death many years later. The WCTU's ultimate goal was constitutional prohibition, and every effort was toward achieving that goal.[8]

what she did. However, many members of the WCTU treated her with coldness and disapproval. Even the WCTU state president, Elizabeth Hutchinson, voiced her disapproval of Nation's actions. Nation pointed out, however, that Governor William Stanley of Kansas had appointed Hutchinson's husband as resident physician of the State Reformatory. Nation believed that Stanley had appointed Hutchinson's husband to this position to thwart his wife's efforts toward the temperance cause.

The state WCTU, however, refused to commend Nation. Hutchinson even wanted Nation to tell a temperance convention meeting in Barber County that the WCTU had no connection with her earlier saloon destruction. The state WCTU officials wanted little to do with Nation.

The convention meeting in Barber County had an impact on the town of Medicine Lodge. Many temperance workers in the town kept asking embarrassing questions involving the illegal sale of alcohol. Because of this, county officials were moved to seek out the bartenders, saloon keepers, and saloon owners and compel them to answer for their "crimes" in court. When these people were brought before the justice of the peace of Moore Township, Moses E. Wright, he found them guilty. The justice was a devout Free Methodist, and he admired Carry

Nation. For the first time since Kansas became a Prohibition state, Barber County was free of saloons.

The people who sold liquor were now so fearful of Nation and of losing their business that they left Medicine Lodge, Kansas, for good—at least until Nation left for other parts of the country later on. Even Nation's enemies admitted that her unusual means of stopping the illegal sale of alcohol often worked. Many people in southern Kansas—where Medicine Lodge and Kiowa were located—praised her. Some temperance advocates, however, disagreed with her violent method. The people who made their living with the manufacture and sale of alcohol were, of course, still strongly against her. But Nation's mind was made up. Given her success in southern Kansas, nothing could stop her from carrying her crusade to other parts of Kansas and the rest of the country.

2

CHILDHOOD

Carry Amelia Moore's childhood contrasts sharply with her later life. She was born on November 25, 1846. Her birthplace was a huge, ten-room, log farmhouse in Garrard County, Kentucky. On the inside were plaster walls, which were somewhat unusual for that time. The house stood on a high cliff above the Dix River in Kentucky. Four stately columns supported the wide front porch in front of the house and gave it an inviting appearance. A walkway lined with cedar trees and decorative bushes led to the front door.[1]

The family maintained the parlor as the special room in the house. The room's gold-flecked wallpaper had a broad and intricate pattern in keeping

with the formal purposes of the room, which was set aside for special occasions. A brass fireplace set enhanced the fireplace, complemented by red plush furniture on a soft carpet. And in one corner of the room, a wooden cabinet held the family books—all except the Bible and certain religious tracts, which were carefully placed on a nearby table. The cabinet was kept locked from Monday to Saturday. A drawn portrait of George Moore, the head of the home, rested on an easel in the room. A portrait of the family head was characteristic of the time, and also showed that the Moore home was one of wealth.

The family kept this room, like many other country parlors of the day, closed off from the rest of the house. The room was used only at special times, such as when the minister came to visit and read a passage from the Bible, or when a family member died and the corpse was displayed for mourners.[2]

Carry's Father

Carry's father, George Moore, took much pride in his Irish ancestors. He was descended from an Irish pioneer who had also lived in Garrard County. Moore had been quite well-to-do until he lost many of his possessions during the Civil War. Although Moore had little education, he was a stock trader and planter. Like many planters at the time, he was

also a slaveholder. When his daughter was born, he wrote her name in the family Bible as Carry Amelia Moore.

Carry loved her father dearly. As a child, her ambition was to be like him in every way. She even tried to wear her teeth down on one side so her teeth would look like his. She later wrote about her father:

> If I ever had an angel on earth, it was my father. I have met many men who had lovable characters, but none equaled him in my estimation. He was not a saint, but a man—one of the noblest works of God. He was impetuous, quick, impatient, but never nervous, could collect himself in a moment and was always master of the situation.[3]

She also called her father a "thorough business man," but said his social manners were his most outstanding qualities.[4]

Carry would accompany her father as he drove to a market in Cincinnati to sell hogs on certain Sundays. In the Christian religion, Sunday is supposed to be for rest, not for work. On one occasion, she told him that he would lose money on the hogs because he was working on a Sunday. Her father replied, "Stop that! Every time you say that, I do lose!"[5] According to Carry, her father did lose money on that particular occasion.

The Campbell Side

Carry's mother was Mary Campbell, a daughter of James Campbell. James Campbell was a native Virginian who claimed to be descended from one of the Dukes of Argyll from England. He claimed also to have been related to General William Campbell, who married Patrick Henry's sister (Patrick Henry was a famous patriot during the American Revolution). He also said he was related to Alexander Campbell, a well-known religious leader who established the church of the Disciples of Christ, later known as the Christian Church.

In his youth, James Campbell worked as a carpenter; but in later years had acquired considerable wealth. He owned numerous slaves and had many acres of rich farmland. In his early twenties, Campbell and a friend, Buckner Miller, moved from Virginia to Kentucky.

Although James Campbell could be very stern, he enjoyed serving and drinking liquor. It was while visiting at her grandfather's that young Carry first encountered alcohol. Each morning at the breakfast table, James Campbell would fill a tall glass with butter, brandy, sugar, and hot water. After thoroughly stirring the mixture, he would ask each person at the breakfast table if he or she would like a taste. He would then give each one a spoonful and drink what was left. The temperance movement

was not well organized at the time. People accepted the practice of drinking liquor by many, even preachers.

Carry's mother, Mary, was several years younger than her husband. Both of Carry's parents had been married before, but both of their mates had died. Although Carry was the Moores' first child, she was not close to her mother and preferred her father's company. As she grew older, Carry considered her mother extravagant and too desirous of gaining social attention. When her husband purchased a new carriage, the driver dressed in broadcloth and a high silk hat. A young male slave jumped off and on the back of the carriage, opening the gates. Young Carry disapproved of such means of display.

Kentucky Bluegrass

The Kentucky bluegrass region is located in the middle of the state of Kentucky. Consisting of roughly eight thousand square miles, the "bluegrass" soil consists of fertile loam (soil consisting of clay, silt, and sand) underlaid with rapidly disintegrating Lexington limestone. The soil contains a high percentage of phosphorus and nitrogen, which helps plants grow. The bluegrass area is part of a larger, rich agricultural area in Kentucky. Because of the abundant nutrition in bluegrass, this area is favorable to raising various livestock, notably horses, that feed on the grass.

Early Schooling

In 1853, when Carry was six, her father sold his Garrard County property and moved with his family and slaves to Danville, Kentucky. A year later, the family moved again to Woodford County, Kentucky, where Carry's father bought a farm between Midway and Versailles. At Midway, Carry began school. She also attended Sunday school for the first time. In later years, she gave much credit to her early Sunday school teacher who faithfully taught her from the Bible.

Carry's father's African-American slaves, with whom she spent much time, probably influenced her mature religious beliefs even more than her Sunday school teachers. Even when she went to regular church services, which were segregated (separated by race) at the time, Carry sat with the African Americans in the balcony. She attended their prayer meetings and other religious activities as well. Their singing and shouting inspired her greatly, and her favorite religious song was "Let Us Sit Down and Chat with the Angels."[6]

Carry experienced her own struggles against sin, too. She said she feared the coming of Judgment Day (the end of the world) when Christians believed all people would stand before God and either be judged good and sent to heaven or evil and sent to hell. Carry would steal anything forbidden in the house, then invent fantastic stories as to how it disappeared. She also took whatever she wanted from her aunts' and her grandfather's houses by opening their boxes and bureau drawers and grabbing money, perfume, powder, silks, ribbons, and laces. Carry made the latter three items into clothes for her dolls.

In spite of repeated scoldings and spankings, Carry continued to lie, steal, and commit other offenses such as mimicking a preacher at graveside services she would hold for a dead cat or bird. Her spiritual life was at a very low point when Carry moved with her family to Belton, in Cass County, Missouri, in 1856, at the age of ten.[7] During the journey, Carry caught a terrible cold, which developed into a more serious illness. She was very ill for nearly a year. During this time, everyone who knew her discussed the possibility of her dying and of her need for spiritual salvation.

After a few weeks of illness, Carry was taken to Sunday school. The preacher gave her a small book that happened to pinpoint her sin of stealing. The book noted that anyone who stole little things was just as much a thief as one who stole items of much value. The book even specified some of the small articles that Carry had been stealing. In short, the book shocked her when she realized she was a thief. In time, she felt cured of dishonesty, stealing, and even selfishness as she attempted to give away many personal items.

After Carry recovered from her illness in 1856, she went with her father to the Christian Church at Hickman's Mill, Missouri. She sensed that the minister directed his words and his gaze right at her, and before she left that day, she went forward in response to the minister's invitation and became a Christian. The next day, she was baptized in a little stream about two miles away. As she came out of the water, Carry felt she enjoyed a new peace.[8]

For the next five years, Carry's health suffered, and she was bedridden much of the time. Because of her physical condition, she rarely entered into normal childhood activities. She became somewhat depressed and found increasing consolation in religion. She memorized numerous passages from the Bible and took much delight in preaching to the slaves—either from a dining room table or, occasionally, from her bed.

Carry's elementary-school education, however, tended to be interrupted frequently. She had attended primary schools in Kentucky, and when she was thirteen, Carry's father sent her to Mrs. Tillery's boarding school in Independence, Missouri. Again, she was able to spend barely a third of her time in the classroom due to frequent illness, and she soon returned home. Her father then hired a

private tutor to teach Carry at home, which turned out to be short lived as well. Her schooling, though irregular, was quite typical for girls in her time. People believed that since girls would most likely marry and raise a family, they did not need much, if any, education.

Her Father's Losses

The plan to have Carry tutored was given up when Carry's father experienced financial setbacks because of trouble between Missouri and Kansas. In

Secession Crisis

On December 20, 1860 (just a few weeks after Abraham Lincoln, who was antislavery, was elected president of the United States), a South Carolina convention called by its legislature voted to secede, or leave, the United States. By February 1, 1861, the southern states of Mississippi, Florida, Alabama, Georgia, and Louisiana had followed suit. A week later at Montgomery, Alabama, a provisional government of the Confederate States of America was established. Texas soon joined the Confederacy. When Fort Sumter, South Carolina (held by Union forces), was fired on by Confederate soldiers on April 12, 1861, the War Between the States, or Civil War, had begun. Within a few days, Virginia, Arkansas, North Carolina, and Tennessee joined the Confederacy, and both the South and the North had begun preparing for the full-scale war that was to come.

addition, the Civil War had begun in 1861 when Carry was fifteen years old. The northern and southern states were at war because of disagreements over slavery (which still existed in the South) and states' rights. Her father's slaves became increasingly unwilling to work because they heard talk about being set free. Finally, he loaded up his family, belongings, and some slaves and livestock and left for Texas. After six weeks of difficult travel, on roads filled with refugees and other migrating families, the Moores stopped in Grayson County, Texas. Carry's father bought a farm and attempted to put in some crops.

Again, disaster plagued him. Many of his horses and mules died before he could plant cotton. Then, an epidemic of typhoid fever broke out among his family and slaves. As many as ten people were ill at one time and several slaves died. Completely discouraged, Moore freed his slaves, sold what property he could, and started back to Missouri in 1862. Enroute to Missouri, the Moores gave bedding and supplies to the wounded soldiers they saw all along the way.

Carry's Father Starts Over

Back in Belton, Missouri, Carry's father discovered that his lands were ruined, his livestock was scattered, and his remaining slaves had disappeared. To

supplement their meager farm income, the family took in boarders. During this time, Carry, now seventeen, spent several months in a boarding school at Liberty, Missouri. Once more, however, she found her education interrupted by her mother's serious illness. Carry became nearly overwhelmed as she did the cooking, cleaning, and laundry for the family. Then, one of the new boarders, Dr. Charles Gloyd, a Civil War veteran who arrived in November 1865 to board at the Moores, changed Carry's life.

3

BLUSHING BRIDE AT TWENTY-ONE

Although Carry Moore's formal schooling appeared to be over, she began to study the Bible with new zeal. Her knowledge of Scripture served her well as she began to teach Sunday school classes, attend church regularly, and participate in prayer meetings. Her father allowed her to attend an occasional country dance, too. However, she refrained from dancing what was known as a "round" dance, or dancing with one partner. Nation remarked about such dancing: "I cannot think this hugging school compatible with a true woman."[1] Some of the books Nation read at the time were Sir Walter Scott's *The Lady of the Lake*, *The Works and Writings of Flavius Josephus* (a Jewish historian at the time of Jesus Christ), and books of mythology and poetry.

As a young woman, Moore was nice looking, with long, dark hair that fell in ringlets on her neck; she had a lovely complexion and an attractive figure. She also possessed the good manners expected of a young lady who was well brought up. She had a quiet demeanor, saving her more boisterous moments for church and prayer meetings.[2] These church services tended to give Moore a feeling that she was doing good, and she looked forward to attending them.

The common method followed for a young woman to find a suitable husband at the time was for a young man to visit the woman in her own home, preferably in the family parlor. Moore had

her share of young suitors seeking her out. When the couple sat in the parlor attempting conversation, she would "read the poets . . . and Scott's writings, and history. Read [Flavius]

Even at a young age, Carry Nation was very interested in religion.

Josephus, mythology and the Bible together."[3]
Having the subject continually turned to these top-
ics must have confused any young man, and after
some light refreshments of cake and lemonade, her
would-be suitors soon left.

Change of Plans

Moore's life took a new turn, however, when her
parents' boarder, Dr. Charles Gloyd, kissed her in a
darkened hallway. Before this incident, she was very
reserved and had not even allowed a man to hold
her hand. She said later: "I had never had a gentle-
man take such a privilege and felt shocked, threw up
my hands to my face, saying several times: 'I am
ruined! I am ruined!'"[4] Gloyd soon asked Moore to
marry him. She found herself in love with the handsome doctor and planned to accept his proposal of
marriage.

Unfortunately, Carry's father was not pleased
with his daughter's plans. He had already chosen
the son of a well-to-do neighboring farmer for her to
marry. Her father discovered that she had made up
her mind. The love notes written by Gloyd and
tucked into a volume of Shakespeare's plays placed
on the breakfast table had completely swayed her.
Moore greatly respected anyone who was well-
educated and who had a good mind. Gloyd met
those requirements. He spoke several languages and

possessed a superior education. She was soon in awe of him, and her reverence for him quickly turned to adoration and love.

Moore's parents tried to warn her that Gloyd was a drunkard, but she paid them little attention. She had never encountered anyone who drank much, except her grandfather who was a moderate drinker.

Moore, like other women of her era, had few opportunities open to her outside of marriage. According to a study of the American frontier, "Marriage was still seen by most Americans as the only appropriate be-all and end-all of a young woman's life. After all, how else could she find love, protection, and the opportunity to fulfill herself through motherhood?"[5]

Some other areas women could work in included those of being laborers, missionaries, or teachers. Moore accepted her role in life as a matter of course. She wished someday to found a "Preparatory School for Women" where women could be taught "to wash, cook, scrub, dress, and talk, to counteract the idea that woman is a toy, pretty doll, with no will power of her own. . . . To be womanly, means strength of character, virtue and a power for good."[6]

Married Life

Moore's marriage to Gloyd took place in Belton, Missouri, in the family parlor, on November 21, 1867.

But when the groom arrived for the ceremony, he was already drunk and stumbled as he pronounced his wedding vows. From that time on, Carry Gloyd scarcely saw him sober. What she thought would be a blissful life with the man she loved, turned out to be much different than she dreamed.

Carry Gloyd had believed that whatever faults her husband had, including drinking to excess, her love for him would effect a cure. However, her husband was a confirmed alcoholic (although people had little understanding of the term then) and continued to drink almost continuously.

At first he told her he had an illness, and she believed him. Within the first week of their marriage, however, she began to realize that alcohol held her husband in its grip. It often transformed him from a loving sweetheart into an angry, difficult husband.

Charles Gloyd seldom came home until after midnight. His medical practice dwindled to nothing, and often there was not enough food to eat. When Carry Gloyd discovered she was going to have a baby, she felt desperate. Night after night, she searched for her husband, often finding him at the Masonic Lodge. The Masons, a private organization, did not permit women on the premises, so all Mrs. Gloyd could do was go home and wait for her husband to return. She sought the church for help but

Masons

A Mason, or "Freemason," is a member of a worldwide fraternal and charitable organization with secret practices and signs. The term also means a person who works with brick or stone, but here, it refers to a member of this organization. Many of the Founding Fathers and early presidents of the United States belonged to the Masonic Order.

got only sympathy. She sat home alone, night after night, weeping and brooding over her disastrous marriage.

When Carry Gloyd's father found out what had happened to his daughter, he came to visit her. Then, realizing she was without even sufficient food and clothing, he insisted she return home with him. She protested bitterly, not wanting to leave her husband.

Her father won out. Carry Gloyd reluctantly left her husband of only a few months to return to her parental home. She was upset over her marriage and her situation. Within a short time, her life would take still another turn.

4

LIFE WITH AN ALCOHOLIC

Once at home with her parents again, Carry Gloyd had time to reflect on her brief married life with Charles Gloyd. Almost from the time they married, her husband seemed to change. She saw that he became sad and gloomy, and was not quite the good husband she hoped he would be.[1] "He was kind but seemed to want to be away from me; used to sit and read when I was so hungry for his caresses and love."[2] Carry Gloyd believed that other young married women experienced a similar situation with their husbands, and she believed that liquor caused it.

Desperate Days

Five days after their wedding, Charles Gloyd came home, laid down on the bed, and fell asleep. Although Carry Gloyd was in an adjoining room, she observed her mother-in-law go over to her son and bend down into his face, as if to confirm that he was drunk (she did not realize that Carry had observed her). A few minutes later, when his mother had left, Carry did the same thing and "the fumes of liquor came in my face."[3] From then on, Carry said she saw no happy moments and cried most of the time.

Charles Gloyd did not intentionally make his wife unhappy, and said on several occasions that he would do whatever necessary to make her happy. However, he seemed to be helpless to do so. Day after day, and night after night, Gloyd neglected his medical practice and stayed away from home much of the time. Carry soon discovered that her husband

Alcoholism

Alcoholism is the continued excessive or compulsive use of alcoholic drinks. The increased use of alcohol leads to chronic and progressive deterioration of the nervous and digestive systems. In particular, the habitual use of alcohol leads to addiction and greatly impairs a person's mental state.

went to the Masonic Lodge to drink, and he refused to see anyone.

As she observed her husband's nightly pattern, Carry Gloyd asked one of the Masons to help her. Then she talked to a good friend, Clara Mize, whom she considered a Christian, and asked for her help. Both people could only say, according to Nation, "Oh, what a pity, to see a man like Dr. Gloyd throw himself away!"[4] To the Masons, who hid and protected Charles Gloyd (and drank with him), his wife was a nuisance: The church, as well, did not reach out to pray against the saloon keepers or pray for Gloyd (as his wife requested). So Carry Gloyd found herself alone with the situation. But her hatred of alcohol was being nurtured, as well as her hatred of tobacco (Gloyd was also a smoker) and her dislike of the Masons because they refused to help her. For the remainder of her life, Carry would speak out against all three of these perceived evils.

Alcoholism

People did not know a great deal about alcoholism during this time, but Dr. Benjamin Rush completed an early study in 1785 on the subject. In this later passage, he discusses the medicinal uses of alcohol as prescribed by a medical doctor:

> So great is the danger of contracting a love for distilled liquors by accustoming the stomach to their stimulus, that as few medicines as possible should be given in

spirituous vehicles, in chronic diseases. A physician of great [importance] . . . [said regretfully] . . . that he had innocently made many [drunks] by prescribing brandy and water in stomach complaints. . . . It is well known several of them died of intemperance [drinking too much] in this city, since the year 1790.[5]

Carry Gloyd knew she was pregnant and could see only more difficult times with her husband once a baby arrived. Back home with her parents, she continued to write her husband daily, for she loved him and still hoped he would change for the better.

Benjamin Rush

Benjamin Rush, an American physician, was born on December 24, 1745. He graduated from Princeton in 1760, and from the University of Edinburgh, Scotland, in 1768. In 1769, he became a professor of chemistry and medicine at the College of Philadelphia. He was active in pre-Revolutionary War movements and signed the Declaration of Independence. He was a delegate to the convention in 1780 that formed the Constitution, and he established the first dispensary in the United States in 1785. In 1787, he became a member of the convention that ratified the Federal Constitution. He was a founder of Dickinson College and an advocate of the abolition of slavery. He was also connected with various religious and scientific societies. From 1797 until his death on April 19, 1813, he served as treasurer of the U.S. Mint.

Her mother told her she could have nothing to do with her husband. Carry knew that if her parents put her out, Charles Gloyd could not support her. She wanted him to sign "the pledge"—a type of vow people would make not to drink alcohol. The following is an example of the pledge:

> *A pledge we make, no wine to take,*
> *Nor brandy red that turns the head,*
> *Nor fiery rum that ruins home,*
> *Nor whiskey hot that makes the sot,*
> *Nor brewers' beer, for that we fear,*
> *And cider, too, will never do;*
> *To quench our thirst we'll always bring*
> *Cold water from the well or spring.*
> *So here we pledge perpetual hate*
> *To all that can intoxicate.*[6]

Charles Gloyd did not reform or sign the pledge. In her parental home, Carry Gloyd's mother insisted again that Carry have nothing more to do with Gloyd. When Gloyd tried to see his wife, coming two times to her parents' home in Belton, Missouri, Mary Moore refused to let him talk to Carry alone. When Carry's daughter, Charlien, was born on September 27, 1868, Moore did not notify Gloyd. Gloyd had no idea that he had a child until the baby was six weeks old, when Carry went back to retrieve her belongings.

Charles Gloyd begged Carry to stay with him, telling her that if she did not, he would not be able

Temperance

To have temperance is to have moderation and self-restraint, especially in eating and drinking. In the eighteenth and nineteenth centuries in America, temperance came to mean restraint or abstinence in the use of alcoholic beverages. As more became known about the evils caused by alcohol, the temperance movement was born. The original aim was toward moderate drinking, but prohibition became the movement's goal.

to control his desire for alcohol. He also said he would be dead within six months if she did not stay with him. She wanted to stay but dared not disobey her parents, who had decided the separation must be permanent. Six months later, Carry Gloyd received a telegram announcing that Charles had died on March 20, 1869. His death was reportedly due to pneumonia made worse by excessive drinking or delirium tremens—confusion and hallucinations with violent shaking caused by prolonged, excessive use of alcohol.[7]

Happiness Returns

When she learned of her husband's death, Carry was very sad. Despite her mother's objections, she went back to Holden, "To be with the mother of the man I loved more than my own life."[8] Gloyd's mother was a widow with no means of support, so Carry was determined to find some way to care for herself, her daughter, and her mother-in-law.

Carry Gloyd took stock of her assets, which consisted of three town lots that her father had given her as a wedding present and her husband's medical library and instruments. She sold these possessions and had a small three-room house built for herself, her daughter, and her mother-in-law. She rented out the larger house where she had lived with Charles Gloyd.

When she realized the rental income was not enough for them to manage on, Carry Gloyd decided to attend the Normal Institute of Warrensburg, Missouri, to become a teacher. She lacked the necessary money, but friends helped with the room and board, and she soon became a student. She was happy to be getting the education she had always wanted. Within a year, she received a teaching certificate. She was hired by the Holden Public School to teach in the primary grade, which she did from 1871 to 1874.

After this length of time, Carry was abruptly dismissed over having her young students pronounce a short *a* instead of a long *a*. A prominent member of the school board had visited her class and objected to the pronunciation. The dismissal over something so trivial seemed ridiculous. The board

member simply found whatever wrong he could find in Carry's teaching so that his niece could have her position. Carry also found herself blacklisted from working in other schools in the area.

Once more, she had no way to earn a living. As she struggled with worry and anxiety over what to do, the thought came to her that she should remarry.

With a new resolve, she prayed: "Lord, you see the situation. I cannot take care of mother and Charlien. I want you to help me. If it be best for me to marry, I will do so. I have no one picked out, but I want you to select the one that you think best."[9]

After praying, Carry Gloyd waited and watched for the right person to appear.

5

MARRIAGE TO DAVID NATION

Roughly ten days after Carry Gloyd prayed for a husband, she returned from the post office on the afternoon of November 6, 1874, and saw David Nation. Nation, a lawyer, minister of the Christian Church, Union veteran, and editor of *The Warrensburg Journal*, had come to Holden that day on business. As Carry Gloyd walked by, he turned and spoke to her. She felt a strange thrill pass through her, as if to confirm that he was the man God wanted her to marry. The next day, she received a courteous letter from him, and a few weeks later, on December 30, 1874, they were married. Though this seems like a short courtship, most historians today believe that Carry and David

Despite an age difference of almost twenty years, David Nation and Carry Gloyd were married on December 30, 1874.

Nation had known each other for a few years before their meeting on the street.[1]

David Nation was nineteen years older than his bride. He generally wore a high-crowned black felt hat, and he had scraggly, flowing whiskers that hung below his chin. His bride considered him quite handsome.

A New Chapter

Carry now came to believe that the spelling of her first name was prophetic. She sensed that her new name, "Carry A. Nation," was an act of God. Following her marriage to David Nation, she wrote, "This does not mean that I will carry a nation, but that the roused heart and conscience of the people will, as I am the roused heart and conscience of the people."[2]

From the outset of their marriage, the Nations had little in common, and their union was characterized by bickering and arguing. Carry believed that her husband deceived her in various ways. He became annoyed by her excessive and rigid Christianity. Although he was a minister, David Nation disapproved of his wife's ideas of reforming mankind. She sensed that her idea of a Christian life offended him. It was not long before she felt that, "if I yielded to his ideas and views I would be false to every true motive."[3] She thought her husband

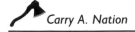

believed that she resented his influence, which led him to become suspicious and jealous. The result of their attitudes toward each other caused Carry Nation to develop a combative nature. She attributed her new attitude to her having to "fight for everything I kept."[4]

In January 1877, the Nations packed up their household furnishings, cattle, horses, and hogs and moved to Brazoria County, Texas. David Nation had bought seventeen hundred acres of land on the San Bernard River and planted some of the acreage in cotton. Their farming venture was disastrous when eight of their nine horses died the first spring, an angry neighbor threw their plows and other farming equipment into the river, and one of their farmhands stole much of their money.

All of these problems caused David Nation to become very discouraged.

He abruptly left whatever crops were still in the field and went to the nearby town of Columbia to practice law. Carry Nation was left to take care of the farm with her daughter, Charlien, who was seven years old; her stepdaughter, Lola Nation, who was eleven; Mrs. Gloyd, her former mother-in-law; and a destitute old man whom the Nations took in out of charity. Carry Nation managed to harvest some of the cotton crop with the help of some African Americans she paid with bedding and articles of furniture. However, she had no way of getting the crop to market.

More Trouble

David Nation had taken the few dollars the family had to pay his room and board in town. Before long, Carry Nation and her family faced starvation. Few of their neighbors reached out to help them. The family lived on corn meal, fat bacon, and sweet potatoes—the only vegetable planted in the garden. The children lacked energy, and Carry Nation was very sick with chills and fever. Once, the family found someone to accept a bushel of potatoes in exchange for sugar, tea, and bread.

As if things could not get worse, after the family had eaten the last of their food, they received word from David Nation that he needed money. Although she could barely walk, Carry got the children and Mrs. Gloyd into an old wagon. With the one remaining horse, they headed for Columbia. They arrived in town late at night and waited in the wagon until the next day when Carry sold some of the cotton crop. Then the family enjoyed a good breakfast.[5]

Managing the Columbia Hotel

Since neither of the Nations could find work in Columbia, Carry began to manage the Columbia Hotel, a run-down building in need of repair, in

1879. She cleaned as much as possible and tried to get rid of the rats and mice. When the hotel opened for business, Carry used the money she made from one meal served to the guests to buy the next meal. She did most of the cooking, worked in the dining room, and kept up with the laundry. Mrs. Gloyd and Lola Nation cleaned, swept, and made beds. David Nation sat at a desk in the hotel office waiting for a client to file a lawsuit or any legal matter with him. He waited in vain, for no one appeared to file a lawsuit or a claim of any kind.

Carry Nation's work was never-ending, and she finally became ill with chronic diarrhea. Nevertheless, she continued her tedious work in the hotel. She had little time to read her Bible or attend church. However, she prayed a lot, and her cries to God could often be heard by those passing by the hotel.

Charlien's Mysterious Illness

In November 1880, Charlien became sick with typhoid fever. When she got better, she began to show symptoms of mental illness. Nation blamed her daughter's problems on herself, because she married someone addicted to alcohol.[6] But even worse, her only child refused to read the Bible or go to church.

Nation asked God to deal drastically with Charlien. She prayed that God would send a physical affliction to Charlien, if that would make her love God and serve Him. Then Charlien's right cheek became swollen and a sore was discovered eating away the inside of her cheek. The doctors could not discover the cause.

Carry Nation prayed earnestly, and the sore healed except for a hole in the cheek the size of a quarter. Charlien's jaws locked and stayed that way for about eight years. Charlien came under the care of a doctor in Houston who operated on her cheek and closed the hole. Her jaws and teeth, however, remained closed. She could be fed through a tube,

Typhoid Fever

Typhoid fever, also known as enteric fever, is an infectious disease caused by *Salmonella typhi*. The disease spreads by way of infected water, milk, or food, which may be contaminated by carriers of the disease employed in food preparation. The disease can be diagnosed by taking blood samples. Some of the symptoms are high fever, drowsiness, diarrhea, and abdominal rash. The symptoms progress to delirium and coma within a few weeks. Today the condition can be treated with antibiotics. When traveling to parts of the world where the disease flourishes, immunization is desirable.

but several teeth had to be removed to make this possible. Within the eight-year period of Charlien's locked jaws, her mother took her to doctors in Galveston, Houston, San Antonio, and New York. Nation paid for the operations by taking out mortgages on the Columbia Hotel. Then, a famous surgeon in Philadelphia, Dr. J. Ewing Mears, operated on Charlien and telegraphed her mother in Texas that the child was "all right."[7] When Nation borrowed four hundred dollars to rush to Philadelphia to see her child, she found that Charlien could open her jaws half an inch and was chewing gum. No explanation for her disease was ever given, but from that time on, Charlien grew progressively better.

On the Move Again

Weary of their struggles to do more than just survive, Carry and David Nation moved to Richmond, Texas, in 1881. David began practicing law, and his wife returned to the hotel business. Now she managed several small cottages and a large wooden house with twenty-one rooms. This time she had considerably more work to do but also operated at more of a profit than at the Columbia Hotel.

Nation often had a heavy heart from all the work she had to do at the hotel. She lacked time to attend church and to read the Bible as she wished. She sensed she was living only to nourish people's physical bodies. Often, she would go upstairs, stretch out on the floor, and cry to God for deliverance from her present surroundings. She told God over and over that "if He would free me, I would do for Him what he couldn't get anyone else to do."[8]

Once, when her father visited her, he said he was saddened because she had to work so hard in the kitchen day and night. He told her he had hoped to be able to leave her some money, then added, "Carry, it seems the Lord has been so hard on you."[9]

Carry told him, however, that she thanked God for her sorrows. She believed that God had sent her whatever was best for her. She said, too, that her father had given her something far better. When he inquired about it, she said, "The memory of a father who never did a dishonourable thing."[10] Her father began to weep and seemed somewhat consoled about his daughter's lot in life.

The heavy workload to which Carry Nation had been subjected, along with her daughter's aversion to Christianity, began to take its toll on her. Her mind began to wander, and she had recurring dreams and visions. She believed that she received messages from angels, and she supposedly conversed with God and Jesus on a regular basis.

Nation had two recurring dreams that she thought were very significant. In one, she dangled over a precipice by a thin rope held by a hand that

came out of a cloud. In the other, she saw two snakes lying in the grass on each side of the road. One of the snakes was huge and full of venom and tried to strike her. The other snake lacked energy and was undernourished. Several years passed before Carry Nation understood the meaning of the dreams. In the first dream, she saw herself as the person dangling over the cliff with God's hand holding on to her. She believed that in the second dream, the venomous snake represented the Republican party while the malnourished snake was the Democratic party. She believed that the Republican party was her enemy. At the beginning of her crusade against alcohol, the Republican party was in power. Nation realized that the liquor industry was government licensed and taxed, so she blamed the Republicans for coming against her.

Spiritual Blessings

On Christmas Eve, 1883, Nation's father, George Moore, died. Shortly after, Nation became so ill that she could not leave her bed for weeks.[11] This period of physical illness was followed by a boost to Nation's spiritual life.

In the summer of 1884, the Methodists held a conference and revival in Richmond, Texas, and Carry Nation attended every preaching session. At one of the early meetings, the minister preached from the sixty-second chapter of Isaiah, which says, "Thou shalt also be a crown of glory in the hand of the Lord and a royal diadem in the hand of thy God" (King James English Bible). These words stirred Carry Nation. She trembled and shook all over, began to weep uncontrollably, and heard wings fluttering in her ears. According to Nation, she saw angels standing in the aisle and a shining halo around the minister's head. Then she supposedly felt the church leave its foundations and float into the skies, and she said she was "caught up into Paradise, and heard . . . [that] which it is not lawful for a man to utter."[12]

When the vision cleared, she looked around the church to see if anyone else had heard or seen anything. Each person seemed unaffected. Nation felt that what she had received was the baptism of the Holy Ghost. From then on, she determined to live completely for God, and to do His bidding. Following her spiritual experience, Nation began telling her friends and everyone she encountered that "from henceforth all my time, means and efforts should be given to God."[13] In all her words and actions from that time, Carry Nation tried to do just what she declared she would.

THE MAKING OF A CRUSADER

While living in the town of Richmond, Texas, Carry Nation taught Sunday school at the Methodist, then the Episcopal, Church. But after her visions, her relationship with both churches changed. She did not belong to the Methodist Church, and the minister objected to her teaching a Sunday school class but not being a member. Later, when she was teaching at the Episcopal Sunday school, the minister came into the classroom and asked why she did not teach the children certain things. She told him that she could not agree to teach that being baptized makes a person a Christian. Both churches thus forbade her to be part of them.

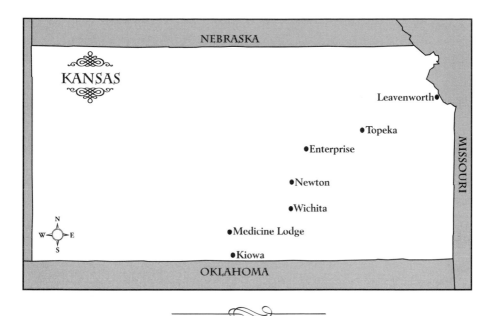

Carry Nation made a name for herself in the state of Kansas. This map of present-day Kansas shows the towns Nation would visit on her crusade against alcohol.

One evening in the winter of 1889, David Nation returned home after being beaten up by members of a political faction.[1] The minister informed his wife that he wanted them to move to Medicine Lodge, Kansas, where his brother Seth lived. David Nation left right away and became a minister at the Campbellite Christian Church in Medicine Lodge. In March 1889, Charlien married Alexander McNabb of Richmond, Texas, at her mother's urging. By then, Charlien had completely recovered from her physical ailments, but her mind was becoming increasingly weak. Carry Nation

stayed in Texas to help with Charlien's wedding, then left for Medicine Lodge to meet her husband. Both Charlien and Lola Nation stayed in Texas.

Following the Nations' move to Kansas, David Nation served at the Campbellite Christian Church for less than a year, disagreed with the church board, and quit his position. While he pastored in the church, however, Carry Nation took an active part in his ministry. Her concern for his ministry began because she did not think he had ever been converted, or was called by God to preach. So she took it upon herself to help him as much as possible. She chose his texts and sometimes edited and wrote his sermons, which usually included attacks on tobacco, alcohol, and other local abuses. She sat in the front row and prompted her husband audibly to lower or raise his voice, to speak faster or slower, and to use more gestures. When she thought the sermon topic had been dealt with, she would step into the aisle and say in a loud voice, "That will be about all for today, David!"[2]

The Town Busybody

Not only did Nation interfere with her husband's preaching, but she became a social busybody, correcting various individuals when she thought they needed correcting. One of her main concerns was perceived sexual misconduct. She stopped young women on the street and warned them not to go buggy (carriage) riding with young men because of the danger of seduction. In Medicine Lodge, when she encountered a young couple sitting closely together, the man's arm around the woman, Nation flew into a rage, telling the man to treat the woman as his sister. Then she told the young woman that ruin would be her fate.

Nation received another vision after she and her husband moved to Medicine Lodge. While the local Baptist minister was visiting Nation, he read from the Bible. As he was reading, a streak of lightning flashed near the house, lighting up the outdoors. Carry Nation thought she saw an outline of angel wings pressed against the windowpane. At the same time, she felt what she called "divine electricity" flowing from her head through her whole body.[3] The Baptist minister quietly left the house, not knowing what to think of the startling event.

Thrilled with this new visitation from God, Carry Nation proceeded to run from house to house shouting to the occupants that the Lord had given her a great blessing. She then urged them to praise and thank God. When she returned to her home and read in the Bible, the very words seemed to light up in a soft glow. As a result of her religious experiences, Nation felt well qualified to dictate her

ideas to the ministers of Medicine Lodge. They, in turn, tried to avoid her whenever possible.

Carry Nation reached out to help the town's poor people and children. At Christmas and Thanksgiving, she would go from house to house with her horse and buggy and ask people for food and clothing to give to the poor. She asked the town merchants to contribute goods. If a merchant refused, she would walk around town proclaiming his stinginess. At prayer meetings, she would beg the Lord to forgive him. The town's poor people greatly loved her, calling her "Mother Nation," but her enemies also referred to her by that name.

Now Carry Nation took the responsibility of many reforms upon herself. She ran up to people and snatched cigarettes from their mouths. She had a long list of things she disliked: Women who dressed well were like "mannikins hung with the filthy rags of fashion." Men belonging to clubs were "diamond-studded, gold-fobbed rummies [(drunks)] whose bodies are reeking masses of corruption."[4] When President McKinley was assassinated in 1901, Nation's diagnosis was that he might have survived had his blood not been poisoned by nicotine, the active drug in the tobacco in cigarettes.

William McKinley

William McKinley was born in Niles, Ohio, in 1843. He was a Republican statesman and the 25th president of the United States. He served in the Civil War, then became an attorney. In 1876, he was elected to Congress, and in 1891 became governor of Ohio. He was elected for two terms as president, in 1896 and again in 1900. A short time after beginning his second term as president, McKinley was shot in Buffalo, New York, on September 6, 1901. He died eight days later.

The "Dry" State of Kansas

Carry Nation had looked forward to living in Kansas where the manufacture and sale of intoxicating beverages had become illegal in 1880. To her amazement, she discovered that as much drinking was carried on in Kansas as in Texas and Missouri. She found that every town and village had its own saloons, known as joints. In addition, many drugstores sold liquor in backrooms or at the front counter as medicine. The law was not enforced because of the political power of the anti-Prohibition forces and the liquor industry.

At first she contented herself to be part of the WCTU and to speak against the places that sold liquor. When she became jail evangelist for the WCTU, however, and saw firsthand the results of

chosen at random. She would close her eyes and stick a pin in the Bible page. When she opened her eyes, the verse stuck with the pin was the one she needed to examine. On June 5, 1900, she found the verse that spoke to her as the leading from God that she needed. The verse was Isaiah 60:1 in the Old Testament and went as follows: "Arise, shine; for thy light is come, and the glory of the Lord is risen upon thee."

Joyfully, Nation ran up and down the streets telling the neighbors a change was coming in her life. She knew her life's purpose would now be fulfilled. As she continued to pray and fast, asking God what to do about the saloons in Kansas, she believed God told her to "Take something in your hands and throw at those places and smash them!"[6]

Carry Nation intended to be obedient to the revelation and do just that. She proceeded to Kiowa, Kansas, in June 1900, to carry out her mission.

Anti-Saloon League of America
The Anti-Saloon League was established in 1895 with the aim of forbidding alcoholic drink by amending the U.S. Constitution and by enacting state and local antialcohol laws. The league eventually became part of the National Temperance League in the 1930s.

Carry Nation had to proceed cautiously because she was unknown. She reported any observed law breaking regarding the sale of alcohol to the county attorney, but he was occupied with other things. When he refused to bother with her, Nation accused him of taking bribes. He sued her for slander, and when the case came to trial a few months later, Nation paid a one-dollar fine. But the trial costs amounted to two hundred dollars, and a lien, or debt, was placed on her home as a result of the trial. She could not pay what she owed until a few years later.

Carry Nation was upset as she observed the increase of saloons and alcohol drinking in Kansas. She knew the situation called for drastic measures. The authorities appeared unwilling to help, so she would call on a higher power. She began to fast and pray, crying out to God to help her close the saloons. At times, she even walked through the streets wearing clothing made from burlap (sackcloth) with ashes sprinkled on her head. The townspeople labeled her as crazy and a fanatic, and, as they had in Medicine Lodge, began to avoid her.

7

THE PRIZE OF WICHITA

The local WCTU greeted Carry Nation as a heroine after her assault on Kiowa.

She had accomplished more to enforce the prohibition laws in six months of saloon smashing than twenty months of ineffectual law enforcement, the churches, and the temperance movement had. Some of the extremists in southern Kansas hailed her as a heroine, while others with a more moderate position disliked the violence she used. The liquor advocates attacked her with new vigor. They spread the rumor that she was insane. Because of the rumor, Nation refrained from telling many people about her visions and directives from God.

While her outward appearance seemed subdued, inwardly Nation desired to push on. As the winter of 1900 came, she held the conviction that perhaps, just as Moses had led the people of Israel to the "promised land," in the Old Testament, she was destined to lead America's people to a promised land of prohibition where no alcoholic beverages existed.

Conquering Wichita

After the trial ended in Kiowa and David Nation had left on a trip to visit his brother, Carry Nation decided it would be a good time for her to prepare to go to Wichita. She chose an iron rod as her new weapon of destruction, but also took some rocks and bricks that she had used earlier. She also took one of her husband's canes and a valise, or small bag, to hold some toilet articles and her Bible. The biggest part of her preparation was the time she spent praying on her knees and studying the Scriptures. She was thrilled to have (as she believed) the words light up with gold. Now she was ready for her next assault.

On December 27, 1900, Nation, dressed in a black alpaca dress and a dark poke bonnet (a woman's hat with a brim in front), got on the train for Wichita. She arrived in the city about 7:00 P.M. and, after registering in a small hotel near the station, decided to survey some joints.

One of the places Carry Nation looked at was the Carey Hotel. Known from coast to coast, the Carey Hotel contained one of the finest bars in the West. The ceiling and walls were made with blocks of fine gray stucco that had decorated buildings at the Chicago World's Fair in 1893. The bar itself, made of cherrywood, was over 50 feet long. All the furnishings and glass were spotless, including the brass rail, the cut-glass decanters, the huge mirror, and the cherry-wood tables.[1]

What caught Nation's eye, however, was the life-size painting of a completely nude woman, Cleopatra, hanging over the bar. Beside her were nude handmaidens, and the two attendants who fanned Cleopatra wore only loincloths. The painting was known as *Cleopatra at the Bath* and had been painted by John Noble. Although the Kansas City *Star* noted the following day that the painting was worth one hundred dollars, it was probably worth considerably more. The artist had worked on it for nine months and later became quite well known because of it. When Nation first looked at the painting, according to witnesses, she let out a "screek," or, as others said, a "shrill, thin 'Yawk!'"[2] She spoke to the bartender, asking, "Young man! What are you doing in this hell-hole?"

"I'm sorry, Madam, but we don't serve ladies," replied the bartender.

Carry Nation quickly gained a reputation as an extremist and some temperance workers thought she hurt their cause more than she helped it.

"Serve me!" Carry Nation yelled. "Do you think I'd drink the hellish poison you've got here? What is that naked woman doing up there?"

"That's only a picture, Madam."

"It's disgraceful!" Carry Nation exclaimed. "You're insulting your mother by having her form stripped naked and hung up in a place where it is not even decent for a woman to be when she has her clothes on!"[3] With that, she turned and walked out the door.

The next day she was back and armed for battle. Nation first threw a rock at the painting. It broke the glass and went through the canvas. The second rock she pitched missed its mark of ruining the painting beyond repair, something that greatly distressed her later. She had determined to cause as much damage as possible to the bar, so her third rock shattered the elegant Venetian glass mirror, worth fifteen hundred dollars. Her first words were heard by the bar patrons: "Glory to God! Peace on earth, good will to men!"[4] Then with the iron rod and cane she had tied together, she continued whacking at everything in sight: glasses, bottles, decanters, the cherry-wood bar itself, the chandelier, and the brass rail.

The bar patrons scattered, some heading for the back door, and the bartender got down on his knees. Just then the police arrived and placed Nation under arrest for destruction of property. She objected, telling the officer that the man who ran the bar was the person to arrest. Nevertheless, she was taken to jail. As she walked off with the officer, she let the onlookers know that when she got out of jail, she would destroy Wichita's other joints. The strains of Carry Nation singing, "Am I a Soldier of the Cross?" could be heard as she headed toward jail.[5] She had done almost three thousand dollars in damage to the Carey Hotel Bar.[6]

Detective Park Massey and the Wichita police chief, G. T. Cubbon, were perplexed about how to charge Carry Nation. Their predicament was similar to that of the police in Kiowa and in Medicine Lodge. They faced the problem of how to charge her with breaking the law and, at the same time, charge the Carey Hotel (and other joints) with breaking the law of serving liquor.

Vindication

During Nation's time in jail, she attempted to get in touch with Governor William Stanley at his home in Wichita by phone. When she could not reach him, she sent him a note. She told him she was being unlawfully deprived of her liberty. The governor read the note over a few times, then replied that he had nothing to say to her. After the governor declined to interfere in her case, County Attorney

Sam B. Amidon decided to prosecute her. On January 5, 1901, she was brought before Judge O. D. Kirk of the city court and charged with malicious destruction of property—the property being somewhat vaguely described as belonging to the Carey Hotel.

As Nation faced the court, she said somewhat defiantly that she would have nothing to do with the court until Amidon put out his cigar. She told him it was rotten and the smell poisoned her. The courtroom crowd snickered, and Amidon, enraged, flung away his cigar. She then asked that the charge be amended to read "destruction of malicious property." When the county attorney objected, she insisted that she would not be tried without her own attorney.[7]

The jailers took the composed Carry Nation to her cell. However, the minute the steel doors clanged shut, she became hysterical and began to cry and moan. She grabbed the bars and tried to loosen them, and cried loudly, "You put me in here a cub, but I will go out a roaring lion, and I will make all hell howl!"[8]

Carry Nation's exploits in the Carey Hotel had already caused quite a stir not only in Wichita, but all over Kansas. Whether people applauded what she did or hated it, they were interested in her. Newspaper reporters, in particular, had suddenly

found a person with much popular appeal. The temperance advocates, too, began to champion her cause. The Wichita chapters of the Woman's Temperance Union and the Kansas State Temperance Union held special prayer meetings, and the Wichita chapter provided a lawyer for Nation. Although Nation did not hear from Elizabeth Hutchinson, the president of the Kansas state WCTU, Lillian Mitchner, the WCTU district president, came from Topeka late in the afternoon. She led a large group of women to the county jail where they sang and

Carry Nation often prayed and read the Bible during her many stays in jail.

prayed in the hall near Nation's cell for several hours. At intervals, Carry Nation shook her cell bars and prayed on her knees and cried out in spasms of religious emotion.

Her stay in jail was quite miserable from a physical standpoint. She got sick with flu and had frequent headaches. Government officials, in an effort to make Nation feel miserable, put prisoners who smoked in cells near hers, knowing that she did not like cigarette or cigar smoke. They also put a mentally ill man in the cell next to hers. Between the smoke she breathed and listening to the poor man next door fall on the floor and moan and curse at intervals, she got little rest or relief. David Nation, returning from his trip, hurried to Wichita

John Brown

John Brown was a militant abolitionist who was born in Torrington, Connecticut, in 1800. In 1859, he led a raid on the U.S. Armory at Harpers Ferry in Virginia with the intention of getting weapons for a planned slave rebellion. The raid failed, and he was convicted of treason. He was hanged at Charlestown, Virginia, in 1859. The song "John Brown's Body" commemorates the Harper's Ferry raid and was sung by Union soldiers during the Civil War.

to see about his wife. He declared that she was not being treated well.

Finally, on January 12, 1901, Carry Nation was released from Sedgwick County jail, and on January 18, all charges against her were dropped by a motion from the county attorney. He told the court that he had much concern for her mental state and could not in good conscience bring Nation to trial. He also thought she could not stand the shock of further confinement.

Carry Nation's stay in jail served only to make her more determined than ever to close down the places that sold liquor in Kansas. She said she was ready, if need be, to sacrifice her life, like the abolitionist John Brown, for the cause she believed in. As she passed through the prison doorway into bright sunshine and saw a good sized crowd of well wishers, she called out: "God's work has only begun!" After a few moments she added, "Show me a joint!"[9]

8

FEARLESS CRUSADER

O nce out of jail, Carry Nation was anxious to get back to the task at hand of smashing joints. Her husband, David, decided that she needed some time to rest, and he persuaded her to come with him to Newton, Kansas, in Harvey County. In Newton, she delivered a temperance speech and rested a few days. On January 21, 1901, she returned to Wichita to her earlier scene of triumph.

A short time after her return, the Wichita WCTU called a special meeting to welcome and praise her. When she spoke to the assembled group, she attacked the saloons and the city officials who refused to close them down. Then she called for those who would accompany her on a smashing crusade and were willing to sacrifice themselves for the Lord.[1] Almost every woman in the group jumped to her feet, eager to accompany Nation on her next crusade. From them, Nation selected Lucy Wilhoite, Julia Evans, and Lydia Muntz.[2]

The Smashing Begins

At the January 21 prayer meeting, the women planned their strategy. They gathered an assortment of weapons: stones wrapped in newspaper, iron bars, and chunks of scrap iron. Nation, for the first time, carried a sharp, gleaming hatchet. Then Nation and the women marched out onto the streets singing "Onward Christian Soldiers," and turned onto Douglas Avenue where James Barnes's saloon was located.[3] Nation led the ladies through the saloon doors, and the people seated at the bar quickly scattered in every direction.

Barnes came toward the women, his arms extended, and said in a pleading voice, "Now ladies."[4]

Disregarding the bartender's plea, Nation yelled, "Don't come near my hatchet! It might fall on you, and I will not be responsible for the results!"[5] With that remark, the hand holding the hatchet swung near the owner's ear, and she urged the "rummy" to get out of her way.

The frightened bar-owner ran for the rear of the saloon. It was all over within fifteen minutes, and

Carry Nation looked upon the triumphant scene of wreckage and thanked God. As Nation and the ladies filed out, they passed by the bewildered owner, James Barnes, and she blessed him as she left. The ladies were very happy. No one had tried to stop them, and a growing crowd of onlookers cheered them on.

The women rushed on down Douglas Avenue to Herrig's Palace Café, which they had chosen as their next stop. Chattering excitedly as they came through the front door, they chased a number of drinkers to the back door and threw several stones at the large mirror and bottles lined up behind the bar. Suddenly, Nation felt the barrel of the owner John Herrig's revolver against her head as he shouted for her and the women to get out. She took his advice. The group then headed for the Carey Hotel where Nation had begun her smashing in Wichita.

By now, most of Wichita knew that Carry Nation was on another rampage. The crowd surrounding the women was growing by the minute as people left their homes and businesses to watch Nation in action. When the women arrived at the Carey Hotel, however, the police had already been summoned. Detective Sutton of the Wichita police force grabbed Nation's arm when she attempted to run past him. She thrust at him with a poker, and an excited young man who had run beside her shouted

frantically, "Hooray for God and Carry Nation!" and hit the detective in the face.[6] He was quickly taken into custody by the police, along with the four women, including Nation. After the chief of police received a promise from the women not to do any more smashing before noon the next day, they were released. Their freedom was short lived, however, as a warrant for their arrest was issued a short time later, and they were taken back into police custody.

While the women rejoiced over being in prison, considering themselves martyrs, or those who sacrifice, for the cause of prohibition, other members of the WCTU were meeting in their homes. They gathered to thank God for the destruction of two more joints in their city. Groups of men were also roaming the streets discussing the day's happenings. A plan began to form as to how to deal with Carry Nation. The talk became violent, and close to midnight, between fifty and one hundred men milled around the county jail yelling and cursing Carry Nation. There was even talk of lynching her. The mob lacked leadership, and when the police told them to leave, they vanished into the night.

The next afternoon, Nation, Lucy Wilhoite, and Julia Evans appeared before the judge of the district court. He ordered them released on bail of one thousand dollars each. The bail was provided by temperance and prohibition workers several hours

Lynching

To lynch someone is to execute that person, often by hanging, without trying the person in court. A "lynch law" calls for the punishment of persons suspected of a crime without a trial. The original "lynch law" was drawn up by Captain William Lynch and a group of neighbors on September 22, 1780, in Pittsylvania County, Virginia. The men wanted to have a way to deal with some lawless men who were disturbing the county's citizens. The courts were thought to be too far away to help, so Captain Lynch and the men took the law into their own hands through their newly conceived "lynch law."

later. Word spread through Wichita that Carry Nation had been freed. When several large insurance companies heard the news, they cancelled accident policies of saloon owners.

Instead of staying in Wichita, Nation went to the railroad station to board a train for Enterprise, a small town of eight hundred in central Kansas. She arrived in Enterprise about seven o'clock in the morning on January 23, 1901, and went to the home of C. B. Hoffman, Sr. In the afternoon several members of the WCTU came, and the ladies held a special prayer and song service. Nation told them she intended to smash the joints of John Schilling and William Shook, and all the women clapped and cheered.

By three o'clock, Carry Nation, accompanied by Catherine Hoffman and Mrs. L. A. Case, left the Hoffman home to speak at a local Methodist Church. Soon, however, she was leading a crowd to the saloons. But the saloon owners had heard that the women were coming and had taken extra precautions against them. Arriving at Schilling's place, Nation found the door locked and bolted. That did not stop her. She made quick work of crashing through the door and into the barroom. A gathering crowd outside cheered and applauded all the proceedings.

Once inside, Nation and the other women smashed the long mirror behind the bar, hit and gashed the bar itself, and broke bottles and decanters behind the bar. The women broke open the locked refrigerator, dragged several cases of beer into the middle of the room, and broke each beer bottle. No one tried to stop the destruction until Marshal W. R. Benham appeared. He gave Nation a shove, and the crowd shouted for him not to treat a woman like that. When he threatened that he would use violence if necessary to prevent further destruction, Nation left, going back to the Hoffman home for the evening.

Carry Nation crashed through the locked door of John Schilling's saloon. A crowd soon gathered as she did more damage inside.

After supper, Carry Nation decided to return to the town business district. There, she began speaking on a street corner. A few minutes into her speech, one of the bar owners, John Schilling, came up to her. He shook his fist in her face, saying, "My wife will settle with you!"[7]

A few minutes later, Belle Schilling rushed at Nation and hit her twice, causing a deep cut over one eye and bruising the other. Nation pursued her attacker without success: Returning to the street corner, she applied a beefsteak to her eye and resumed her talk. She exclaimed to her listeners: "I want to suffer! I am ready to die for the cause! I am merely an instrument in God's hands!"[8]

The following day, January 24, 1901, Nation, Hoffman, and several other women went to William Shook's saloon. There, they received a promise from Shook to close his business. As they left the place, Nation once again encountered John Schilling, who repeated his warning to her about his wife's getting

The marshal of Enterprise escorts Carry Nation away from the destruction she caused in town.

even with her. No sooner had he warned her than several rotten eggs were thrown at her. Then, while John Schilling held Nation down, four women he had hired and a few companions rushed at Nation with whips, heavy rawhide thongs, and thick tree limbs. Carry Nation was no match for this vicious attack. One woman struck her repeatedly with a whip, another lashed her shoulders with the rawhide, and a third grabbed her long hair and pulled out a huge handful. With that, a woman gave Nation a big push, and she fell into the gutter where the women proceeded to beat and kick her.

Even Nation's cries for help from other women nearby went unanswered until an old woman with a brick in her hand rushed up to threaten Nation's attackers. They ran off. Nation was helped to her feet and into the carriage. She returned to the Hoffman home and recovered after a few days. She then decided to leave Enterprise. The assault on Nation roused much anger toward her attackers and much popular support toward Nation. Both the opposition against and the support for Carry Nation would increase considerably in the days ahead.

CARRY NATION GAINS NATIONAL FAME

As Carry Nation arrived in Topeka, Kansas, on January 26, 1901, she told reporters that she would no longer attack saloons by herself. She intended to organize Mothers' and Sisters' Clubs all over America. Her plan was that members of these clubs would pledge themselves to continue smashing campaigns and to cause trouble in their family circles if their husbands and sons frequented barrooms. Triumphantly, she told the reporters: "Within a year we will clear the nation of hell-holes!"[1] By "hell-holes," Nation meant the saloons and barrooms that she was so against.

After smashing John Shilling's saloon in Enterprise (above), Carry nation set her sights on Topeka.

Topeka's Importance

Topeka was the capital of Kansas and headquarters for the liquor lobbies, and also for temperance leaders. Compared to Wichita, Topeka did a much better job of enforcing prohibition laws. The city had about forty saloons (for thirty-five thousand people), but in very few were beer and whiskey served over standard bars with actual barroom equipment. Most of the saloon keepers had antiquated equipment such as old iceboxes and plain board counters. They kept their supplies tucked away in back rooms behind restaurants or cigar stores. None of the saloons operated openly, and the city had fewer wholesale and storage warehouses than Wichita did.[2]

The person most responsible for Topeka's good prohibition rating was Police Chief Frank M. Stahl. Stahl, himself a temperance advocate, seemed tireless in enforcing Kansas's prohibition laws. Of course, the liquor interests in Topeka regarded Stahl with resentment, but they treated him amiably because they hoped the Kansas legislature would pass more liberal legislation regarding the liquor interests.

When Carry Nation stepped down from her train in Topeka, a newspaper reporter described her:

> The first thing I noticed when I saw her was how terrible her clothes were—quite worn out. She had on a shiny black dress with a fringed gray shawl . . . her shoes seemed pitifully thin and worn. . . . Everything she wore, though, was clean and mended, and her humorous face had something of the shine of her clothes as if it, too, were being perpetually scrubbed and polished.[3]

Nation's friends and supporters had urged her to take more care with her dress, but clothes that were clean and mended satisfied her.

The Reverend S. C. Coblentz of the United Brethren Church met Nation at the station, and after she gave a short speech, the two left for Reverend Coblentz's home. In less than an hour, however, Nation was back on Topeka streets wanting to look at its joints. She traveled first to the *Capital* offices, the city's leading newspaper, where she demanded to be escorted to the saloons. The people in charge at the offices were indifferent to her since most of the city's reporters already surrounded her, and she had no need of any further escort.

The first place Nation visited was Bert Russell's billiard hall. When the men playing pool looked up and saw her entering the door, they made a dash for the back room. The back door slammed, and she stood banging on the door, commanding someone to open it in the name of God and American motherhood. Suddenly Edward Ryan, one of Russell's managers, picked her up and carried her out the front door. She protested, but he told her to stay out.

The next joint was closed, so Carry Nation went on to Edward Myers's cigar store. Myers's place was also closed, and his wife walked back and forth in front of it carrying a heavy broom. She warned Nation not to come any closer. Nation told her to get out of her way, that she was going into her "murder-mill."[4] With that, Nation shoved Myers aside.

A second later, Myers struck her on the head with the broom. The pile of hair on top of Carry Nation's head broke the force of the blow, but her bonnet got knocked off into the gutter. As she stooped to pick it up, Myers struck her again.

Nation began to cry loudly and run down the street with Myers in pursuit. Two blocks later, reporters expressed their sympathy. Nation retorted, "What does a broomstick amount to when one has been used to rawhides, rocks and eggs? Where is another joint?"[5]

The Crowd Turns Ugly

By now a crowd of about two thousand followed Nation. The next place she visited was a chili parlor. The owner was friendly and offered her a free meal, which she refused. A thorough search on her part revealed no sign of liquor in the chili parlor.

Meanwhile, as Carry Nation went back out into the street, the crowd's mood had shifted. The policemen with her were few in number. When someone threw a rotten egg at Nation, then some small stones, those in charge became concerned. They hurried Nation to another location of her choosing, the *Capital* newspaper offices. She had chosen the offices as her unofficial headquarters. The newspaper's special officer, George Luster,

went to the door with a revolver to disperse the crowd, which had even spoken of lynching Nation.

Carry Nation was not a person to back down. In a short time, she went back outside. Sensing the crowd's attitude, however, she quickly got into a carriage and rode to the Columbia Building where the deputy city attorney, D. H. Gregg, was waiting. When the crowd still pursued Nation and continued to speak of lynching, the Columbia Building custodian was called to deal with them. He went after the crowd holding a revolver in each hand, and at last, the crowd withdrew from the premises. Nation noted as she left a few minutes later that her work for the night was finished.

Victory in Topeka

On Sunday, January 27, 1901, Nation's second day in Topeka, a large crowd gathered in front of the Reverend Coblentz's home. The crowd waited for something exciting to happen. Whenever someone glimpsed Carry Nation at a window or door, the crowd cheered wildly.

Nation's husband, David, arrived from Medicine Lodge that day and wished for her to come home with him. He failed to understand why his wife did what she did in "this saloon smashing business," as he said.[6] He added that his wife fasted for days sometimes, and he had to force her to eat. He stated that she talked with an unseen being who she

> claimed was Christ. . . . When she smashed the saloons at Kiowa she came home all covered with blood . . . she had only cut her hands on broken bottles. . . . she said the Lord would heal her wounds, and, sure enough, in a day's time there was not one scar left.[7]

Carry Nation called on some of the leading politicians—state and local. She failed to meet with most of them but did see Governor Stanley. He told her that if she got the prosecuting attorneys in various counties to put the joint owners in jail, he would do his best to keep them there.

Following this visit, she tried to reach Police Chief Frank M. Stahl, who was unavailable. He said later, however, that he supported Carry Nation, even if her methods were violent. If the state officers did their duty, Stahl added, Nation would not have to do what she did.

The state Temperance Union's annual convention began the following day, Monday, January 28, 1901, in Topeka. The convention delegates were divided over Nation's violent method of closing saloons. Some believed that it was the only way to achieve results. Others said that more gentle, persuasive methods would be better. When Nation's companions ushered her to the front of the convention meeting on January 29, wild cheers went up for her.

She had not been scheduled to speak. In fact, the convention leaders let it be known that her help would not be needed at the meeting.

At the time of Nation's arrival, Catherine Hoffman, one of her coworkers from the Enterprise saloon smashing, was speaking at the podium. Hoffman put her notes aside; began praising Carry Nation; and very quickly, Nation was escorted to the stage. Given a new opportunity, Nation urged her listeners to destroy all the joints in Topeka and beyond. She spoke against Governor William Stanley, saying he had shown a wavering attitude toward the liquor dealers. When she finished speaking, Colonel J. B. Cook of Chetopa, Kansas, suggested that the delegates raise money to give Carry Nation a medal for her efforts. The delegates wholeheartedly approved the idea, and within minutes $117.50 had been raised. A few days later a committee pinned on Nation's chest a gold medal inscribed: "To the Bravest Woman in Kansas."[8]

For a few days, Nation contented herself with speeches against the joints and with setting up her organization, called the Home Defenders Army. The "army" consisted of organized "hatchet brigades" that were led by "drill sergeants" Lucy Wilhoite and Mary Sheriff.

On the afternoon of February 4, 1901, Nation set out with several other crusaders to go saloon smashing at a place called Murphy's Unique Restaurant on Sixth Street. Carry Nation and her companions began their assault but were soon rebuffed by several guards hired by Murphy to defend his place. In fact, more than fifty men attacked the band of crusaders. Nation was hit, kicked, and beaten while the other women escaped. Once more, an angry mob called for a rope and a lynching of the saloon smasher.

If Nation had not been rescued by two policemen, the mob might have killed her. Now, the policemen arrested her and took her to jail.

An hour later, the police wanted to take Nation before Judge Charles A. Magaw, but she would have nothing to do with him. She said that if she was to appear in his courtroom, the police would have to carry her there. Judge Magaw then released her.[9] Once released, Nation promptly went to a hardware store with several friends and bought thirty new hatchets. They would soon come in handy. Carry Nation and her crusaders engaged in other barroom skirmishes in Topeka, with huge crowds of people following Nation even in times of winter weather.

On February 5, 1901, Nation and her companions visited the Senate Bar, one of the finest saloons in Topeka and a favorite with state politicians. Nation and the other women wrecked the saloon.

Then, a policeman entered the premises, arrested Nation, and took her to jail. This time, appearing before Judge Magaw again, Nation was charged with inciting a riot. The judge asked her if she pled guilty and she said no. She did say, though, that she smashed a joint. She was released on one hundred dollars bail, the case being postponed until February 7.

On February 6, the Topeka Police raided several saloons and closed them down in response to Nation's efforts. And while she spoke to a crowd in front of the post office, a man ran up to her and gave her several small pewter hatchets. He told her to sell them to the crowd, so she could pay her expenses. From that day on, Nation carried a good supply of souvenir hatchets and was able to pay most of her expenses from the money she earned.

When Nation appeared before Judge Magaw on February 7, she expected to go to jail. Much to her surprise, all charges were dropped by order of the city attorney. He said there was no city ordinance for which she could be prosecuted. There was no law against wrecking joints. Carry Nation broke into a joyous song with this news, and a happy crowd of admirers followed her out of the courtroom. She led them to the state capitol where she addressed both branches of the Kansas legislature and earned much enthusiasm from many of those present.

A New Direction

These various successes for Nation turned into a profitable venture for her. As she was planning another saloon raid, she met A. C. Rankin, a professional temperance lecturer. He offered to pay her seven hundred dollars to go on a speech-making tour of Des Moines, Omaha, Chicago, and other cities. He told her that if she went on the raid, she took the chance of being arrested again. If that happened, she would lose the money he offered plus the opportunity to deliver her message to other places.

Carry Nation jumped at the chance, and on February 8, 1901, she left Topeka in the company of Rankin; Reverend F. W. Emerson; and several women, including Madeline Southard. Southard, at twenty-four, was already a well-known WCTU lecturer. When she first heard Nation speak in Topeka, she was delighted with both Nation's message and her method of putting saloons out of business. From then on, Southard became an avid follower of Nation.

Nation's tour led her through southwestern Iowa, and big crowds in many small towns such as Stuart, Atlantic, and Adair greeted her as a heroine. Crowds in Des Moines, too, were friendly to her. Because of her great welcome, she at first announced her plans to smash a saloon or two. But when the chief of police told her that she would be

locked up and prosecuted to the full extent of the law—for barrooms operated legally in Des Moines—she changed her mind.

Although enthusiastic crowds greeted Nation, they failed to pay money to hear her speak. So Rankin declared the tour an artistic success but a financial failure and returned to Topeka. Nation and her female companions, however, decided to continue the tour and went on to Chicago.

Nation arrived in Chicago, Illinois, on February 12, 1901. There, the mayor, Carter Harrison, refused to see Carry Nation and sent a warning to her that she must not smash any saloons. Nation walked the streets for a number of hours. The only saloon she entered was Henry McCall's barroom. When a reporter pointed out a nude statue in the window, Nation became furious, stalked inside, and demanded that the manager cover the statue. He did so, putting flimsy pink netting over it along with a sign:

DRAPED!
By Request Of
MRS. CARRY NATION
of Kansas.[10]

Nation ended her lecture tour after visiting Chicago. She used the money she earned to pay off her father's debts. She returned to Topeka on the morning of February 14. She would be surprised at what had happened since her absence.

LASTING ACCOMPLISHMENTS

By the time she returned to Topeka, Nation found a city on the brink of reform. The city had made a tremendous effort to close its saloons. Although Nation desired to get involved in a smashing crusade, she was urged to wait because all the saloons had been ordered to close by city officials. Most of the saloons did close; however, the problem was not solved. Instead of getting rid of their equipment, saloon owners stored it in various buildings and planned to wait for the right time to reinstall what they needed to operate again. It was discovered on the night of February 15, 1901, that the barroom equipment and the whiskey stocks had not left the city as was supposed, but were stored

Carry Nation visited saloons all over the country. Even places with innocent sounding names like the Temperance Hotel did not escape her cautious eye.

instead. The public was outraged over this disregard for the law.

Nation took advantage of the public sentiment and immediately made plans for a raid on the hidden equipment and supplies. From six o'clock in the morning until twilight on February 17, the sound of smashing fixtures, glass, and furniture resounded throughout Topeka. A huge group of volunteers, including college students, marched with Nation. As they finished the work at day's end, Nation was arrested and taken to the Topeka jail.

Carry Nation was arraigned in the district court on February 18 before Judge Hazen. He demanded that she post a bond of two thousand dollars to keep the peace. When she refused, he sent her to the county jail. She told him that God would take care of her.

Publishing Venture

During her time in jail, Carry Nation started her first newsletter, called *The Smasher's Mail*. When she sold ten cows for $240, she put the money into publishing the paper. She had arranged with an African-American man, Nick Chiles, to handle the printing at the plant of *The Kansas Plaindealer*. On February 21, 1901, the first edition appeared locally. The paper contained essays and editorials by Nation, poems, and letters she received. In most of

the essays and editorials, she denounced the liquor traffic. Some of the letters were favorable and supportive, while others criticized her efforts. Some were simply spoofs. After nearly a year of publishing, Nation stopped printing the paper on December 5, 1901.

On the Road Again

The Topeka city authorities decided against prosecuting Carry Nation in court, but she still faced a charge of malicious mischief. This charge had been issued when she entered and smashed the Senate Bar. Judge McCabe, however, dismissed the charge on February 21, 1901, holding that she had shown no special malice toward the owners of the Senate Bar and that she was simply a public nuisance.

Judge Hazen, on the other hand, disregarded Judge McCabe's decision and sent Nation to the county jail. Nation refused to post bond. This meant she had to stay in jail and could not continue smashing activities. Finally, she changed her mind. She had another opportunity from W. A. Brubaker, a professional prohibition lecturer, to travel and speak in Peoria, Illinois, as well as edit an issue of the *Peoria Journal* newspaper. She was released from jail on February 27 when several friends helped with her bond money.

During the long trip from Kansas to Illinois, Carry Nation developed a habit of breaking into train cars where smoking was allowed and dressing rooms where she smelled liquor and jerking cigars and cigarettes from men's mouths.

Nation also complained that her manager, W. A. Brubaker, had destroyed and altered the copy of the *Peoria Journal* that she edited, by placing whiskey and tobacco ads in her copy. The saloons and refineries, where liquor was made, each invited her to stop in and have a drink. Brubaker was not at all what he pretended to be. He turned out to be an anti-prohibitionist and exploited Carry Nation on the tour. She was furious over what Brubaker had done in misrepresenting her. Later she issued a statement denouncing him.

Nation spoke to a large crowd on the night of February 27 at the Peoria Opera House. Afterward, encouraged by reporters, she visited Pete Weise's saloon. She told him of the many drugged and depraved men and women made that way by alcohol. When she objected to a statue of naked women that he displayed, Weise said he would have it boarded up—and he did the next day. A month later, he sent Nation fifty dollars to help with her expenses.

Brigades and Clubs

In addition to her Home Defenders Army, Carry Nation also organized Carry Nation Clubs, which were scattered around the country. Her Home Defenders Army's hatchet brigade continued to make organized attacks on saloons throughout Kansas. Under Lucy Wilhoite and Mary Sheriff, the hatchet brigade demolished numerous saloons in southern and southeastern Kansas. Later on, these brigades, led by women such as Myra McHenry, Rose Hudson, and Emma Denney, smashed saloons all over Kansas, making it one of the leading prohibitionist states in the Union.

Return From Peoria

Carry Nation returned to Topeka from speaking in Peoria, Illinois, on March 1, 1901. On her return, her bond was canceled immediately and she went directly to jail. A large group of Home Defenders Army and WCTU members escorted her to her cell. They reassured her that if any joint rose up during her imprisonment, they would tend to it. When newspaper reporters asked about her plans, she told them, "You just tell the people that Carry Nation will attend to her knitting."[1]

Ten days later, Nation had had enough of her jail stay. Her bail was posted and she was released late in the afternoon of March 11, 1901. She told

Elizabeth Cady Stanton

Elizabeth Cady Stanton was born in Johnstown, New York, in 1815. She studied at Troy Female Seminary in New York. She became involved in the antislavery and temperance movements, and in 1840 married the abolitionist Henry B. Stanton. She was personally responsible for the emergence of women's suffrage as a public issue, but she regarded women's rights as a much larger problem. She supported Carry Nation's "hatchetations" in Kansas. Stanton died in 1902.

reporters at the time that she intended to obey the judge's decree that she could not do any smashing. She felt confident, however, since the judge's restrictions did not apply to Masonry or tobacco, two of her other enemies. Just after being freed, she snatched cigars from the mouths of three men standing in the hallway, and warned them about the satanic character of Masonry. She had not even learned whether they were Masons. One man had never heard of the Masonic Order.[7]

A Shift in Attitude

After her release from jail, Nation's earlier activities seemed to be no longer needed. When she called for a meeting of her former cohorts and those interested in a return to smashing, there was little response. On March 12, 1901, the scheduled meeting day,

only eleven women and one man came. Further
annoyance came when the group failed to endorse
the candidacy of Reverend F. W. Emerson for mayor
of Topeka. For the first time, Nation could not stir
the reformers. Even though she held a few more
meetings in Topeka, the response stayed the same.
So she decided to take her message to other places
in the United States and to Canada and Europe.

A Wide Range

Nation was not a person to stay discouraged about
her lack of support in Topeka or anywhere else.

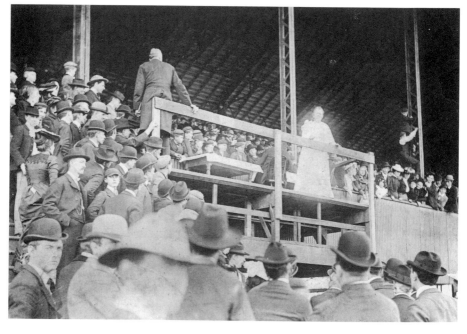

*As a popular temperance advocate, Carry Nation often made
speaking engagements.*

Other people needed her expertise. When she received a letter from the Old Soldiers' Home in Leavenworth, Kansas, asking her to come, she left almost at once. The letter read: "For God's sake come to the Old Soldiers' Home and save the Old Veterans. Bring your hatchet along and clear out the canteen in the Home. . . . Over seventy half-barrels of beer are sold in one day in the Home on Pension Day."[3]

After her arrival at the Old Soldiers' Home, she gave a rousing speech to some aged veterans who then sang hymns with her. As they continued to sing, they led Nation toward the street, where some younger veterans jumped on her and threw her into the street. She was furious and hurried to the center of town to the National Hotel. Bursting into the bar area, she shouted, "Look out for me, you hell-hound, rum-soaked rummies!"[4] The saloon keeper pretended to let her lead him in prayer, but later, when she boarded the train for St. Louis, he reopened his bar.

She traveled from Leavenworth to St. Louis, Missouri, then to Cincinnati, Ohio, and back to Kentucky. In each of these places, she rebuked people for their lack of morals and their drinking habits, and she frequently told smokers, "I want all you hellions to quit puffing that hell-fume into God's clean air!"[5]

In St. Louis, Nation encountered a saloon called The Carry Nation Bar. She strode into the saloon

demanding, "You take that sign down . . . or I'll use a little hatchetation on you!"[6] The owner, Joseph Sauerburger, agreed, but when she returned to the city and his saloon some weeks later, the sign was still there. As she rushed into the saloon, Sauerburger held a pistol up to her and pushed her toward the street.

In the following days and weeks, Nation was in and out of jail in Topeka and Kansas City, Missouri. She was arrested for a number of charges such as blocking traffic and causing a crowd to collect. In Kansas City, she was fined five hundred dollars, but the judge said the fine would be dismissed if she would leave town by a certain time, which she did.

Carry Nation returned to Topeka on July 24, 1901, and she went to the district court where Judge Hazen sentenced her for an earlier charge. He fined her one hundred dollars and gave her a thirty-day jail sentence. After ten days she was miserable. She disliked the food so much that she arranged for a milk man to deliver milk to her jail cell. This entire time she had very little money, although she did receive a small income from editions of *The Smasher's Mail*. She also, however, received notice of numerous bills she owed. These debts greatly troubled her, and she wanted to pay them as soon as possible.

The posters for Carry Nation's tour under James Furlong read: "The Famous and Original Bar Room Smasher." On these particular posters her first name was spelled "Carrie" instead of "Carry."

When she received an offer from James E. Furlong, head of a lecturing tour bureau of Rochester, New York, to take a tour of the Chautauqua circuits in the eastern United States, she was overjoyed at the opportunity. Some friends persuaded Governor Stanley to excuse Nation from her jail sentence and allow her to make small monthly payments on her fine. Her friends also collected money for her, and she was soon off on the Santa Fe railroad.

The first place she spoke was in Clarksburg, Ohio; then she went on to New York City, lecturing at Carnegie Hall and Coney Island. Everywhere she went, she stopped at saloons and scolded people for their habits. In Buffalo, New York, she said to a priest who was smoking, "What a shame for a man to dress like a saint and to smell like a devil!"[7]

Carry Nation brought her 1901 lecturing tour to New York City.

Carry Nation takes time out from her 1901 lecturing tour to pose for this group photo in Rochester, New York.

When Nation returned to Medicine Lodge, Kansas, in November 1901, she received word that David Nation had sued for divorce earlier in the year on grounds of cruelty and desertion. The case was heard in November of that year. In addition to the charges of cruelty and desertion, Nation's husband stated that she had taken his featherbed and some money from his checking account. The featherbed, Carry Nation explained, was hers. She also planned to fight for some of her husband's pension money, which he received as a Civil War veteran. In the end, the divorce was granted in November on the grounds of only desertion, and the property was

equally divided. David Nation, however, got to keep all of his pension.

David Nation also got a piece of property, and Carry Nation got the house in Medicine Lodge, which she later sold for eight hundred dollars. About her husband, she said, "David isn't a bad fellow, but he is too slow for me."[8] At his death two years later, she stated, "I shall meet him on that day when the secrets of all hearts shall be made manifest."[9]

In 1904, Alex McNabb had Nation's daughter, Charlien, judged by a doctor to be insane and put in a private sanitarium at San Antonio, Texas.[10] McNabb wrote Carry Nation that he planned to place his wife in a state institution as soon as possible. Carry Nation, however, had other plans for her only daughter. She hurried to San Antonio only to find that Charlien had been transferred to the State Lunatic Asylum at Austin, Texas, on October 13, 1904. Nation was able to secure her daughter's release and sent her to live with relatives in Oklahoma in December 1905.

In the following years, she wrote her autobiography, *The Use and Need of the Life of Carry A. Nation*, published in 1905, and a temperance play, *The War on Drink*. She even did some acting after taking some lessons. She also established a Home for Drunkards' Wives and Mothers. She continued speaking in many different places: college campuses; Nebraska City, Nebraska; Elizabethtown, Kentucky (where a saloon keeper broke a chair over her head); Butte, Montana; Canada; and Europe.

In the late fall of 1905, Nation bought the Harvest Home Mission in Guthrie, Oklahoma, where she installed a printing press to print her publications. She began publication of a new paper called *The Hatchet*. During this time, she lectured in Denver, Colorado, and later on, in Texas. *The Hatchet* was similar to *The Smasher's Mail* in its makeup and editorial policy, but it contained fewer letters and more articles and biblical quotations. The front page of each issue had a large picture of Nation.

The Hatchet was the official newsletter of the Prohibition Federation, with subscriptions selling for twenty-five cents a year. It soon boasted fifteen thousand subscriptions, making it a profitable venture for Carry Nation. Unfortunately for her, she tended to give money and support to the numerous temperance and other professional reformers. She quickly parted with her money.

Nation was given a five-year use of a furnished apartment in Washington, D.C., in 1907, and she proudly declared that the nation's capital would be her new home. Her activities during this time were similar to her early "hatchetation" days. She took

comfort in carrying her three trusty hatchets—Faith, Hope, and Charity—wherever she went. Nation named the hatchets after a New Testament passage in First Corinthians 13:13. Those three qualities would remain, she believed, when everything else failed. She always had a satchel filled with *The Smasher's Mail* and souvenir hatchets, which she sold at a good profit.

Further Activities and Travels

Nation's magazine, *The Hatchet*, was denied mailing privileges in July 1906 because of a letter she had written that was considered obscene. Later, the letter was declared not obscene by a U.S. commissioner in Dallas, Texas. The U.S. attorney said that there was no cause for prosecution.

In Nebraska City, Nation was punched by a bartender, and at Trinidad, Colorado, a saloon keeper threw her out of a saloon. The saloon keeper's shove was so rough, Nation swallowed her false teeth, coughed them up, and broke them.[11] When Nation visited May Malloy's Dance Hall and Cafe in Butte, Montana, May Malloy herself threw her out.

Travels Abroad

While living in Washington, D.C., in 1908, Nation attended the national Prohibition party convention as a delegate. The convention was held in

Columbus, Ohio, where she met Edwin Scryngeour from Dundee, Scotland. Scryngeour was in America studying the anti-liquor movement and invited Nation to visit the British Isles. So, she planned a crusade in Scotland in the fall under the Scottish temperance societies. She agreed to pay her own expenses, and she would receive two thirds of the proceeds of her lectures and other public appearances.

She left New York on the steamship *Columbia* on November 22, 1908, with her niece, Callie Moore, from Kansas City, Missouri. En route to Scotland, Nation managed to smash a mirror in the ship's bar and tried to prevent the use of alcohol by her fellow passengers. Arriving in Glasgow, Scotland, she gave her first lecture a short time later, and on December 17, she was thrown out of a Scottish barroom.

For the next three months, Nation toured Scotland, England, and Ireland. Her activities and speeches were quite similar to those she had given in the United States. The British press took a great interest in her, particularly writing about her in comic magazines. Throughout the British Isles, however, the temperance and prohibition organizations delighted in her.

After lecturing in various Scottish cities such as Edinburgh and Aberdeen, Nation left for England.

Toward the end of her life, Carry Nation traveled overseas to deliver her speeches in favor of temperance.

At Newcastle-on-Tyne, she was arrested for breaking the fixtures in a pub. The officials released her with a warning. Following this part of her tour, she traveled to Cambridge University where she bewildered the students with her American accent and incredible vocabulary.[12]

Although large crowds turned out to hear Carry Nation speak in London, they were often irritated with her. Instead of addressing only crowds in favor of prohibition, she went to speak where she believed people needed to hear her message. While she was onstage, people threw vegetables and rotten eggs at her. She was arrested several times, too, for things such as breaking the glass over a cigarette advertisement on a London underground train. She paid a five-shilling fine and was released.

Nation sailed back to America in March 1909 on the steamship *Dublin*. She found much drinking on this ship, even among the women passengers. As a result, she complained to the captain. He asked that the stewards (ship's attendants) stop carrying liquor to the women passengers.

Semiretirement

While Nation was gone, her property in Oklahoma had greatly increased in value. She sold it on her return and had enough money to buy new property and build a small house in Arkansas, in the Ozark

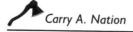

Mountains. She said she had always wanted to live in the country, where she could enjoy the vegetables, flowers, and animals she had enjoyed in her younger days.

In spite of her desire for time to enjoy country life, Nation planned a speaking tour from early July to the end of August for thirty Chautauqua lectures. This time, Sam Holladay of the Midland Bureau of Des Moines, Iowa, had scheduled her.

After she gave her thirty lectures, Nation traveled to New York where she was arrested in early November and fined ten dollars. Her crime was entering and attempting to smash fixtures in the Knickerbocker Hotel Bar and other drinking places in the city.

From New York, she went to Washington, D.C., and on December 8, 1909, she entered a Union Station saloon where she smashed a number of fixtures and glassware. Once more, she was arrested and fined one hundred dollars. The police also kept her three hatchets—Faith, Hope, and Charity.

Final Days

Now sixty-four years old, Carry Nation attempted a short speaking tour in the summer of 1910, but her physical strength was poor. Her speeches had now become pathetic imitations of her earlier tirades against alcohol. She soon had to leave her tour and return to the seclusion of her Arkansas mountain home.

Even reading the Bible had now become a chore, due to her blurred vision and lack of concentration. She also suffered from memory lapses. Nevertheless, she tried to make a final series of speeches against the liquor traffic in the winter of 1911. On January 13, 1911, she made her last public appearance at Basin Park, Arkansas. For a few moments all went well. Her speech was halting but clear. Then she stopped, and a look of confusion and suffering came over her. She raised her hand to her forehead, paused, and said in a stammering voice, "I have done what I could."[13]

Leaving the stage, Nation collapsed into the arms of a friend. She was taken to the Evergreen Hospital in Leavenworth, Kansas. For five months she lay in a hospital bed, lacking energy. On June 9, 1911, Carry Nation died peacefully with just her doctor and a nurse at her bedside. She was buried beside her mother in Belton, Missouri.

Some years later, her portrait and a hatchet that the police had taken were put in the archives of the Kansas State Historical Society at Topeka. A memorial fountain was also put on the spot where Nation was first arrested in Wichita. Her grave, however, remained unmarked until 1923. At that time, her neighbors and friends collected the money

Carry Nation's grave did not receive a marker until 1924, thirteen years after her death.

to erect a granite marker, and on May 30, 1924, the monument was dedicated by the Carry A. Nation Monument Association. The monument was inscribed:

CARRY A. NATION
1846–1911
Faithful to the Cause of Prohibition
"She Hath Done What She Could."

The monument was fitting to one who devoted her life to a cause she believed in. She had indeed "Done what she could."

11

CARRY NATION'S LEGACY

Few people today have heard of Carry Nation, but in the early 1900s, her name was known in almost every small town and city across the United States. Nation's method of dealing with the liquor problem that existed at the turn of the twentieth century set her apart from others involved in both the temperance and prohibition movements.

Before Carry Nation began smashing joints, liquor was available on every street corner in a "dry" state. Although Nation's methods were unconventional and somewhat violent, they called attention to an ever-increasing problem: that of easy access to liquor. She was determined to do something to stop the liquor traffic in Kansas.

Her heartache over her first husband's alcoholism provided Nation with a reason to hate liquor. She said,

> The man I loved and married brought to me bitter grief. . . . I now see why God saw in me a great lover, and in order to have me use that love for Him, and others, He did not let me have those that would have narrowed my life down to my own selfish wishes. Oh! the grief He has sent me! Oh! the fiery trials! Oh! the shattered hopes![1]

Carry Nation's activities opened the way for the Anti-Saloon League to increase in power. In its time, the league had much political influence. Although Carry Nation's methods were crude and involved physical force, she got lawmakers' attention and roused citizens to action. Through what she did, she put a public face on a national issue and caused headlines to focus on the problems of alcohol.

Because of Nation's influence and power, the Kansas legislature voted to stop a program catering to liquor interests. Instead, they approved a measure making "common nuisances" of every liquor establishment.[2] In addition, "it became a penal offense to be found where liquor was dispensed," and a person could be arrested for offering a drink.[3] Her work was often copied, but her supporters felt that no one measured up to her in energy and fame. Many WCTU members became irritated with her at times, but some willingly admitted that she got results in the temperance effort where their methods often achieved little.

Newspaper reporters followed her, hoping to make headlines once more with her activities, which often ended with Nation being jailed. Even in foreign countries like England and Scotland, Nation saw the inside of jails because of the outlandish things she did. She developed her own technique with a hatchet and enjoyed slicing the blade all the way across a row of bottles as if she were using a scythe (a tool used to cut down grass or grains).

As proof of her fame, people from all over the world sent Nation hatchets. Her huge collection included some made of gold and silver. She loved to have children follow her. She would take shiny new hatchets from her bag, give them to the children, and show them how to use them. She also taught them to call saloons "hell holes and murder shops," and liquor "hell-broth and devil soup."[4] As an object lesson to the children, Nation would take them on a saloon-smashing trip where they would wreck saloon interiors and come back with their clothes reeking of spilled liquor.

Carry Nation disliked other habits as well. She was against smoking and often jerked cigars and cigarettes from offenders' mouths. She also railed against fashionably dressed women.[5] Her intense dislike, too, of Masons and the Masonic Order was

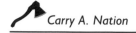

well known, going back to the fact that her first, drunkard husband was a Mason.

Carry Nation was a sometime member of the WCTU but did not always follow its methods. She took the law into her own hands, beginning at Kiowa, Kansas, and later at Medicine Lodge, Kansas, in her early attempts at joint smashing. She called herself a loving "home defender" in her attempts to make the American home free from the menace of alcohol. The WCTU also considered itself an organization of motherhood and purity, and members wore white ribbons to show their affiliation with temperance.

Carry Nation's hatchetation, or joint-smashing displays, helped pave the way for the passage of the Eighteenth Amendment to the U.S. Constitution. The amendment stated that one year from January 29, 1919, all transportation, importation, and exportation of liquor for beverage purposes in the United States would be prohibited. Then, on January 29, 1920, the era of Prohibition came into being in the United States. Thirteen years later, on December 5, 1933, the Twenty-first Amendment brought about the end of Prohibition. Thirty-six states voted to repeal the Eighteenth Amendment. Prohibition had been repealed because it was blamed for high crime and unemployment. People also thought it gave the federal government too much power and deprived immigrants of following the traditions of their former countries.

Because she died in 1911, Carry Nation did not live to see the passage of the Eighteenth Amendment in 1920. Her work was finished at the time of her death as she mentioned in some of her last recorded words. Without her saloon smashing, it is uncertain whether the Eighteenth Amendment would ever have passed. While she lived, she had a profound effect on the moral and political climate of the United States. As one of her biographers said of her, "She, more than any other one person, transformed it [prohibition] from an apologetic weakling into a militant giant of overwhelming power."[6] Nation went to her grave having achieved her goal of alerting the public and lawmakers to the evils of alcohol. She had done all she could; it was up to those who followed to finish her efforts.

CHRONOLOGY

1846—Born on November 25, in Garrard County, Kentucky.

1850s—Attends Kentucky primary schools.

1856—Develops serious illness after moving to Belton, Missouri; Converts and is baptized.

1859—Begins attending Mrs. Tillery's Boarding School at Independence, Missouri.

1865—Civil war veteran Charles Gloyd arrives to board with the Moores.

1867—Marries Dr. Charles Gloyd on November 21 in Belton, Missouri.

1868—Her only child, Charlien, is born on September 27.

1869—Charles Gloyd dies on March 20; Prohibition party founded in the United States.

1871 –1874—Teaches the primary grade at the Holden Public School in Missouri.

1874—Marries second husband, David Nation, a lawyer and minister on December 20; Women's Christian Temperance Union (WCTU) is founded.

1879—Begins managing the Columbia Hotel in Columbia, Texas.

1880—Manufacture and sale of intoxicating beverages becomes illegal in Kansas.

1881—Begins managing a hotel in Richmond, Texas.

1883—Father, George Moore, dies on Christmas Eve.

1884—Claims to have had her first vision.

1889—Charlien marries Alexander McNabb; Carry and David Nation move to Medicine Lodge, Kansas.

1890s—Forms chapter of the WCTU in Medicine Lodge with Kate Cain.

1894—Prays and sings with Kate Cain in front of Mart Strong's saloon in Medicine Lodge; Her efforts lead to the closing of saloons in Medicine Lodge.

1895—Elected president of the Barber County, Kansas, chapter of the WCTU.

1900—Finds a significant Bible passage on June 5, and realizes a change is coming in her life; Smashes first saloon at Kiowa, Kansas; Goes to Wichita, Kansas, December 27 and smashes Carey Hotel Bar.

1901—Arrives in Topeka, Kansas, January 26; smashes saloons and attends WCTU convention where she receives a medal that reads "To the Bravest Woman in Kansas"; Organizes Home Defenders Army in Topeka, Kansas; Starts first lecture tour on February 8, taking her to Iowa and Illinois; Begins publishing newspaper, *The Smasher's Mail*, on February 21; Arrested in Kansas City, Kansas, on March 15; Invited to speak at Leavenworth, Kansas, at Old Soldiers' Home on March 24; Leaves on Chautauqua circuit speech tour, organized by Furlong Lyceum Company, on July 20; Sued for divorce by David Nation in November on grounds of desertion and cruelty. (The court granted the divorce on desertion only.)

1905—Autobiography *The Use and Need of the Life of Carry A. Nation* is published; Begins publishing the prohibition newsletter *The Hatchet* in Guthrie in present-day Oklahoma.

1907—Speaks in Convention Hall, Washington, D.C., to six thousand people.

1908—Attends national Prohibition party convention; Arranges lecture trip to the British Isles and leaves on November 22.

1911—Makes her last public appearance on January 13 in Basin Park, Arkansas; Dies at Leavenworth, Kansas, hospital on June 9, at age sixty-five.

1924—Grave marker is dedicated on May 30.

CHAPTER NOTES

Chapter 1. Saloon Smashing

1. Herbert Asbury, *Carry Nation* (New York: Alfred A. Knopf, 1929), p. 87.

2. Ishbel Ross, *Charmers and Cranks* (New York: Harper & Row, 1965), p. 81.

3. Asbury, p. 88.

4. Ibid., p. 89.

5. Larry D. Underwood, *Love and Glory* (Lincoln, Neb.: Media Publishing, 1991), p. 148.

6. Ibid., p. 149.

7. Ibid.

8. John Kobler, *Ardent Spirits* (New York: G.P. Putnam's Sons, 1973), pp. 136–137.

Chapter 2. Childhood

1. Herbert Asbury, *Carry Nation* (New York: Alfred A. Knopf, 1929), p. 3.

2. Carry A. Nation, *The Use and Need of the Life of Carry A. Nation* (Topeka, Kans.: F.M. Steves, 1905), p. 9.

3. Ibid., p. 16.

4. Ibid., p. 17.

5. Asbury, p. 7.

6. Ibid., p. 13.

7. Fran Grace, *Carry A. Nation: Retelling the Life* (Bloomington: Indiana University Press, 2001), p. 28.

8. Asbury, p. 17.

Chapter 3. Blushing Bride at Twenty-one

1. Ishbel Ross, *Charmers and Cranks* (New York: Harper & Row, 1965), p. 177.

2. Ibid., p. 177.

3. Robert Lewis Taylor, *Vessel of Wrath* (New York: New American Library, 1966), p. 50.

4. Carry A. Nation, *The Use and Need of the Life of Carry A. Nation* (Topeka, Kans.: F.M. Steves, 1905), p. 34.

5. Glenda Riley, *Frontierswomen* (Ames: Iowa State University Press, 1981), p. 5.

6. Nation, p. 30.

Chapter 4. Life With an Alcoholic

1. Herbert Asbury, *Carry Nation* (New York: Alfred A. Knopf, 1929), p. 29.

2. Carry A. Nation, *The Use and Need of the Life of Carry A. Nation* (Topeka, Kans.: F.M. Steves, 1905), p. 29.

3. Ibid., p. 36.

4. Ibid., p. 37.

5. John Kobler, *Ardent Spirits* (New York: G.P. Putnam's Sons, 1973), pp. 43–44.

6. Ibid., p. 131.

7. Fran Grace, *Carry A. Nation: Retelling the Life* (Bloomington: Indiana University Press, 2001), p. 48.

8. Asbury, pp. 32–33.

9. Robert Lewis Taylor, *Vessel of Wrath* (New York: New American Library, 1966), p. 60.

Chapter 5. Marriage to David Nation

1. Fran Grace, *Carry A. Nation: Retelling the Life* (Bloomington: Indiana University Press, 2001), p. 56.

2. Herbert Asbury, *Carry Nation* (New York: Alfred A. Knopf, 1929), p. 6.

3. Ibid., p. 35.

4. Ibid.

5. Ibid., p. 39.

6. Grace, p. 75.

7. Asbury, p. 43.

8. Carry A. Nation, *The Use and Need of the Life of Carry A. Nation* (Topeka, Kans.: F.M. Steves, 1905), p. 46.

9. Ibid., p. 7.

10. Ibid., p. 8.

11. Grace, p. 78.

12. Asbury, p. 48.

13. Nation, p. 47.

Chapter 6. The Making of a Crusader

1. Fran Grace, *Carry A. Nation: Retelling the Life* (Bloomington: Indiana University Press, 2001), p. 87.

2. Herbert Asbury, *Carry Nation* (New York: Alfred A. Knopf, 1929), p. 55.

3. Ibid., p. 57.

4. Larry D. Underwood, *Love and Glory* (Lincoln, Neb.: Media Publishing, 1991), pp. 156–157.

5. Ibid., p. 157.

6. Asbury, p. 84.

Chapter 7. The Prize of Wichita

1. Robert Lewis Taylor, *Vessel of Wrath* (New York: New American Library, 1966), p. 130.

2. Ibid., p. 132.

3. Ibid., p. 134.

4. Herbert Asbury, *Carry Nation* (New York: Alfred A. Knopf, 1929), p. 103.

5. Ibid., p. 105.

6. Fran Grace, *Carry A. Nation: Retelling the Life* (Bloomington: Indiana University Press, 2001), p. 151.

7. Ibid., p. 152.

8. Carry Nation, *The Use and Need of the Life of Carry A. Nation* (Topeka, Kans.: F.M. Steves, 1905), p. 78.

9. Asbury, p. 118.

Chapter 8. Fearless Crusader

1. Herbert Asbury, *Carry Nation* (New York: Alfred A. Knopf, 1929), p. 118.

2. Fran Grace, *Carry A. Nation: Retelling the Life* (Bloomington: Indiana University Press, 2001), p. 155.

3. Larry D. Underwood, *Love and Glory* (Lincoln, Neb.: Media Publishing, 1991), p. 160.

4. Ibid.

5. Ibid.

6. Asbury, p. 122.

7. Ibid., p. 132.

8. Ibid., p. 133.

Chapter 9. Carry Nation Gains National Fame

1. Herbert Asbury, *Carry Nation* (New York: Alfred A. Knopf, 1929), p. 139.

2. Ibid., pp. 140–141.

3. Robert Lewis Taylor, *Vessel of Wrath* (New York: New American Library, 1966), p. 211.

4. Asbury, p. 144.

5. Ibid.

6. Taylor, p. 217.

7. Ibid.

8. Asbury, p. 150.

9. Ibid., p. 158.

10. Ibid., p. 171.

Chapter 10. Lasting Accomplishments

1. Herbert Asbury, *Carry Nation* (New York: Alfred A. Knopf, 1929), p. 195.

2. Robert Lewis Taylor, *Vessel of Wrath* (New York: New American Library, 1966), p. 272.

3. Ibid., p. 298.

4. Ibid.

5. Ibid., p. 299.

6. Ibid.

7. Larry D. Underwood, *Love and Glory* (Lincoln, Neb.: Media Publishing, 1991), p. 164.

8. Ibid.

9. Ibid.

10. Fran Grace, *Carry A. Nation: Retelling the Life* (Bloomington: Indiana University Press, 2001), p. 250.

11. Underwood, p. 165.

12. Asbury, p. 301.

13. Grace, p. 274.

Chapter 11. Carry Nation's Legacy

1. Andrew Sinclair, *Era of Excess* (New York: Harper & Row, 1964), p. 56.

2. Ishbel Ross, *Charmers and Cranks* (New York: Harper & Row, 1965), p. 194.

3. Ibid.

4. Ibid.

5. Ibid.

6. John Kobler, *Ardent Spirits* (New York: G.P. Putnam's Sons, 1973), p. 154.

GLOSSARY

alcoholism—The continued excessive or compulsive use of alcoholic drinks.

alpaca—A thin cloth made of or containing wool from an animal called an alpaca.

blacklist—A list of persons or organizations that have incurred disapproval or suspicion or are to be boycotted or otherwise penalized.

Confederacy—The eleven Southern states that seceded from the United States in 1860 and 1861; a union of persons, parties, or states.

crusade—A series of actions taken for a cause or against an abuse.

devout—Extremely devoted to an idea or belief.

dry—Used to describe alcohol-free states, counties, or establishments; a person who does not drink alcoholic beverages.

emancipate—To free or liberate from bondage, oppression, or restraint.

evangelist—Person who preaches the beliefs of Christianity and tries to convert others.

extremist—One who is so devoted to a cause that he or she takes extreme, sometimes law-breaking, measures to deliver his or her message.

joint—A bar, often where illegal liquor is sold; a saloon.

Judgment Day—In the Christian religion, the day at the end of the world when God judges all human beings, sending those who are good to heaven and those who are evil to hell.

loam—Soil consisting of clay, silt, and sand.

lynch—To execute, often by hanging, without trying the person in court.

prohibition—Ban on the sale and manufacture of all alcoholic beverages. Many temperance advocates favored prohibition.

remonstrance—Earnest presentation of reasons for opposition.

rummy—A drunk.

statute—A law, or decree, enacted by a legislature.

tarry—Linger in expectation.

temperance—Moderation or self-restraint; restraint or abstinence in the use of alcoholic beverages.

tirade—A long, emotionally driven speech.

typhoid fever—Infectious disease caused by *Salmonella typhi*. Symptoms can include fever, drowsiness, diarrhea, a rash, delirium, and coma.

vandalize—To destroy or deface property on purpose.

zeal—Enthusiastic devotion to a cause, an ideal, or a goal.

FURTHER READING

Books

Altman, Linda Jacobs. *Decade That Roared*. Brookfield, Conn.: Twenty-First Century Books, 1997.

Cohen, Daniel. *Prohibition: America Makes Alcohol Illegal*. Brookfield, Conn.: Millbrook Press, 1995.

Cooke, Frank E. *Carrie*. Santa Barbara, Calif.: Fiesta City Publishers, 1995.

Lucas, Eileen. *The Eighteenth and Twenty-First Amendments: Alcohol—Prohibition and Repeal*. Springfield, N.J.: Enslow Publishers, Inc., 1998.

Internet Addresses

"Carry Nation Festival." n.d. <http://www.carrynation.com/carryindex.htm>.

Kansas State Historical Society. "Carry Nation's Purse." *Cool Things*. © 2000. <http://www.kshs.org/cool/coolpurs.htm>.

Nation, Carry A. "The Use and Need of the Life of Carry A. Nation." *Schaffer Library of Drug Policy*. 1905. <http://www.druglibrary.org/schaffer/history/e1900/cn/index.htm>.

INDEX